The
Winning Streak

The Winning Streak

Britain's top companies reveal
their formulas for success

Walter Goldsmith and
David Clutterbuck

Weidenfeld and Nicolson
London

First published in Great Britain by
George Weidenfeld & Nicolson Limited
91 Clapham High Street
London SW4 7TA

ISBN 0 297 78469 2

Typeset and printed in Great Britain
at The Pitman Press, Bath

Contents

The cast

Bernard Audley, *Chairman*	**AGB Research**
Sir Derrick Holden-Brown, *Chairman*	**Allied-Lyons**
Noel Stockdale, *Chairman*	**Associated Dairies Group**
Sir Lawrie Barratt, *Chairman*	**Barratt Developments**
Bill Perry, *Joint Managing Director*	**Bejam Group**
Dick Giordano, *Group Chief Executive*	**The BOC Group**
Sir Owen Green, *Managing Director*	**BTR**
Brian Nelson, *Group Managing Director*	**H.P. Bulmer Holdings**
Daniel Clark, *Chairman*	**C. & J. Clark**
Sir Kenneth Cork, *former Senior Partner*	**Cork Gully**
Lord Weinstock, *Managing Director*	**The General Electric Company (GEC)**
Stanley Grinstead, *Chairman*	**Grand Metropolitan**
Lord Hanson, *Chairman*	**Hanson Trust**
Lord Sieff of Brimpton, *Chairman* (until July 1984)	**Marks & Spencer (M&S)**
Derek Hunt, *Managing Director*	**MFI Furniture Group**
Ian MacGregor, *Chairman*	**National Coal Board**
Sir John Clark, *Chairman*	**The Plessey Company**
Peter Pritchard, *Chairman*	**Pritchard Services Group**
Sir Ernest Harrison, *Chairman*	**Racal Electronics**
Maurice Saatchi, *Director*	**Saatchi & Saatchi Company**
Sir John Sainsbury, *Chairman*	**Sainsbury J.**
Sir Kenneth Corfield, *Chairman*	**Standard Telephones and Cables (STC)**
Sir Nigel Broackes, *Chairman*	**Trafalgar House**
Lord Forte of Ripley, *Chairman*	**Trusthouse Forte (THF)**
Sir Hector Laing, *Chairman*	**United Biscuits Group**
John Beckett, *Chairman*	**Woolworth Group**

The successful companies

AGB Research has grown from very small beginnings in 1962, when it was founded by Bernard Audley, Douglas Brown, Dick Gapper and Martin Maddan MP. Twenty-two years on, the company is not only the largest UK market research company but a provider of information on an international scale with more than a hundred subsidiary companies spanning some twenty countries.

Quoted on the London Stock Exchange, and with a market capitalization in excess of £100 million, AGB has a worldwide staff of 4000 and approximately the same number of shareholders. The company has increased its turnover and profit in every year since it was created.

Today AGB is a diversified information group with interests in trade and technical publishing, computer bureaux and systems, conferences, exhibitions and marketing and consultancy services.

Allied-Lyons is the parent of a group of companies in the United Kingdom and overseas operating within three divisions: beer (Allied Breweries Limited); wines, spirits and soft drinks (Showerings, Vine Products & Whiteways Limited); and food (J. Lyons & Company Limited). The operating companies, many of them household names, are concerned with manufacturing, marketing and distributing a wide range of branded food and drink products both nationally and internationally.

A steady rather than spectacular performer, it has turned around the troubled Lyons group, acquired in the late 1970s.

Associated Dairies Group, Leeds-based, is one of the foremost growth companies in the UK, serving more than 2.5 million British families a week with household essentials including groceries, fresh foods, carpets, curtains, furniture and bedding. The company is also a major manufacturer of meat and dairy products.

Employing more than 29,000 people and with more than 220 retail outlets throughout the UK, the group pioneered the concept of the superstore in the late 1960s with the introduction of its Asda Superstores. Today, most major food retailers are following ADG's example. Group turnover is now in excess of £1.5 billion a year.

Barratt Developments is Britain's largest builder of private houses. Formed in 1958, the company has grown steadily, partly by acquisition, and partly by organic growth, throughout Great Britain. In 1980 the Group made its first venture overseas with the formation of Barratt American and the acquisition of two Californian housebuilders, and is now one of the largest housebuilders in California.

The forty-two subsidiaries which comprise the Group are each profit centres in their own right, and the authority delegated to them is the exemplification of the Group's ideal of the harnessing of entrepreneurial management within the disciplines demanded by public company status.

Housebuilding remains the cornerstone of the Group, but increasing involvement in the total 'shelter' business, including property investment, contracting and leisure property has led to an increase of over 10,000 per cent in turnover during the last decade.

Bejam Group was started by John Apthorp in 1968 with £20,000, a good idea and two colleagues who believed in it. The idea was that the British would soon come to see freezing as the best means of preserving food, particularly if a wider range of frozen food was made available in a more sensible form. It became a public company in 1972, oversubscribed some 132 times. Currently it operates over 200 Freezer Food Centres throughout the UK with a turnover around £300 million in food, and leads the market in the sale of freezers. It employs some 5000 people, is capitalized at over £150 million, and the good idea still occupies the attention of two out of the three originators.

The BOC Group, although based in the UK, now contributes to the economies of some fifty countries throughout the world. In each of these countries, it manufactures as well as markets one or more of its four major product lines: industrial gases, health care, carbon-based products and welding. In all of these products, the Group is either a world leader or among the world's major producers. Additionally, the Group has other businesses involved in vacuum engineering, carbide, educational and food services.

Of its 1983 turnover of £2 billion, over 40 per cent came from the US. Since 1979 the Group's operating profit has risen almost 50 per cent to £153 million and its capital employed has almost doubled to £1.9 billion.

BTR is a diversified holding company with interests in energy and engineering, materials handling, transportation, defence and construction. Sales and earnings have increased steadily every year for almost twenty years, with profits growing at at least 20 per cent a year for the past ten years.

H.P. Bulmer's cider business was founded in Hereford in 1887 and although the company became a public company in 1970, the Bulmer family still own 54 per cent of the ordinary shares. The main business remains cider, occupying about half of the UK cider market, which has now grown to the equivalent of about 5 per cent of the UK beer market. Bulmer's cider is also produced and sold in Australia. Other activities include the wholesale distribution in the UK of wines, spirits and other drinks, including such famous brands as the Domecq sherries and Perrier natural spring water. The company is also the sole producer in the UK of pectin, a natural gelling agent extracted from fruit, used mainly in the jam and confectionery industries.

The company is in the forefront of developments in the field of employee participation, including employee profit-sharing schemes, and has an excellent industrial relations record.

Over the five years to April 1983 turnover increased from £40.4 million to £89 million and pre-tax profits from £2.6 million to £13.3 million through internally generated growth. This performance was reflected in an increase in the ordinary share price by approximately seven times over this period, to give a current market capitalization of £115 million.

C. & J. Clark owns factories in four continents, shops in eight countries and sells throughout the world – not only shoes but the machinery that makes them, the components that go into them and the accessories that go with them. It is a company whose trading objectives are to operate within all aspects of the shoe trade, to do so with the maximum density that is profitable in each of certain chosen territories and to develop export sales elsewhere, where and when possible and profitable.

The chosen territories are the more developed and richer countries for which their products are, in the main, designed and specified. The aspects of the shoe trade in which they operate are supplies to the shoemaking industry, shoe manufacture and shoe distribution, wholesale and retail.

Net sales in the last ten years have risen from £110 million to £511 million, and the trading profit before taxation from £6 million to £27 million. The growth of the company over the past ten years has been in overseas acquisitions and a deliberate expansion of the retail side of the business from 200 shops in 1973 to 1440 shops in 1983.

The General Electric Company (GEC) is Britain's largest electronics and electrical company.

In 1963, when Lord Weinstock became Managing Director, GEC's sales were £131 million and profits were £6 million. Twenty years later, in 1983, GEC's turnover reached £5456 million and profits £670 million.

In addition to about 120 subsidiary companies in the United Kingdom, GEC has manufacturing and selling companies in many parts of the world. Exports from the UK in 1983 exceeded £1000 million. Principal activities of GEC are: electronic systems and components, telecommunications and business systems, automation and control, medical equipment, power generation, electrical equipment and consumer products.

Grand Metropolitan is a UK-based company trading internationally in the food, drink and leisure sectors. Its interests cover brewing, pubs, restaurants, leisure outlets, catering, holidays, milk and dairy products, hotels, wines and spirits, pet foods, sporting goods and tobacco products. In 1983 sales exceeded £4460 million, with total employees numbering around 130,000 worldwide.

Hanson Trust is a leading industrial management company. With 1983 sales of £1.5 billion and major interests in the US as well as the UK, its activities range from building materials, dry cell batteries, department stores and duty-free shops to speciality textiles, engineering and electrical products, footwear, food products and services. The origins of Hanson Trust go back to a small public company then valued at less than £1 million with which Mr James Hanson (now Lord Hanson) and his colleague Mr Gordon White (now Sir Gordon White, KBE) became associated in 1965. It has an unbroken twenty-year record of annually increasing profit, earnings per share and dividends. Pre-tax profit has risen from £10 million in 1974 to over £90 million in 1983, and for the past five years its earnings growth has been one of the highest among £1-billion companies. Since 1984 Hanson Trust has been one of the thirty constituents of the FT Industrial Ordinary Share Index.

Marks & Spencer (M&S), celebrating its Centenary in 1984, is one of the most profitable high street retailers. Lord Sieff, grandson of Michael Marks and Chairman since 1972, relinquished his position as Chairman during the Centenary year and became President of the Company. The Lord Rayner is now Chairman.

Marks and Spencer has a national reputation for the high standard and good value of its product, its policy of good human relations at work and its commitment to buying British whenever possible. Many other companies in this survey referred to aiming to become 'the Marks & Spencer of our sector'.

MFI Furniture Group started as a mail order house and quickly developed into a retail chain specializing in low-price, 'flat-pack' furniture. It now has more than 120 stores across the country. It continues to dominate the flat-pack market and its policy of not delivering goods has led it to become the leading retailer of car roof racks. Turnover in the past five years has trebled, profits before tax have risen by 250 per cent. Sales per employee have risen steadily, reaching £100,000 per employee in 1983.

The Plessey Company is an international organization operating in the fields of telecommunications and office systems, defence electronic systems and equipment, integrated circuit design and manufacture, optoelectronic and microwave devices, small high-performance micro-computer-based systems and electronic components.

Profit before tax over the past five years has trebled from £46.3 million to £146.4 million, while turnover has risen from £648 million to £1075 million.

Pritchard Services Group, originally best known as a UK cleaning company, has not only grown tenfold in the last decade from a £33 million turnover in 1974 to £325 million in 1983, but has also diversified the services it offers through some seventy operating companies in four continents. Health-care services to hospitals and private patients, at £128 million, now exceeds building, cleaning and maintenance, at £117 million; while food services, security services and textile rental, making up the not inconsiderable balance of £80 million, are major forces in the markets in which they operate.

The **Racal Electronics** Group began in the early 1950s as a two-man consultancy. It has shown unprecedented growth, by internal expansion and acquisition, and has become a major international high-technology organization specializing in communications and electronics and is looking for £1 billion in turnover in its twenty-fourth year as a public company. The basic philosophy behind its success is the establishment of small individual companies, each responsible for the design, development and marketing of their own products and service. There are over 100 principal operating companies in the United Kingdom, North and South America, Europe, Asia, Africa and Australia. Over 70 per cent of Racal's products are sold regularly outside the United Kingdom.

Saatchi & Saatchi Company is the holding company for an international network of advertising agencies. It was founded in August 1970 and has grown continuously, becoming the largest agency in Britain in 1980, the largest in Europe in 1981, and figures for 1983 now show it to be the seventh largest network in the world. In 1983 the group employed more than 3000 people in its three main operating divisions – UK, US and international.

Progress up the agency league tables has been more than matched by the company's financial performance. Commission and fee income and profit before taxation have grown without interruption during the company's history, the former growing at a compound annual average rate of 38 per cent per annum, the latter at 47 per cent per annum.

This success can only be attributed to the single-minded pursuit of a consistent strategic goal: the creation of a large agency, with all the stability that gives to employees and all the back-up that provides for clients, but one which at the same time also succeeds in being progressive, youthful and innovative in approach.

J. Sainsbury is a multiple food retailing chain founded in 1869. The present Chairman, Sir John Sainsbury, is a great-grandson of the founder.

Sainsbury traded as a private company until its public flotation on the London Stock Exchange in 1973.

Sir John Sainsbury has commented: 'In the ten years since we became a public company, we have invested £600 million, improved productivity by 44 per cent and created 24,000 new jobs. Profits before profit-sharing have grown from £14 million to £107 million; and earnings per share, adjusted for inflation, have shown a compound *real* growth of 8.8 per cent per annum, one of the very highest among large companies.'

Standard Telephones and Cables (STC) serves the international market for electronics products and services. In 1983 the company turned over £920 million and made a profit before tax of over £92 million. Overseas sales totalled over £270 million. STC is the world's largest supplier of submarine cable systems; but the company also sells internationally competitive products across the whole field of information technology, components, systems and end-user products. Founded in 1883 by Western Electric, it was acquired by ITT in 1925. ITT reduced its shareholding to 35 per cent in 1982. STC has retained a technological agreement which gives it access to ITT's huge worldwide research and development programmes.

Trafalgar House is a first-generation company founded by Sir Nigel Broackes, then a young man. Building on a beginning in property, Trafalgar House went public in 1963 and quickly expanded, at first by acquisition, into building and construction-related activities including such well-known names as Trollope & Colls, Cementation (which itself had absorbed Cleveland Bridge & Engineering), Cunard, and Redpath Dorman Long, bought from British Steel, and most recently Scott Lithgow, also bought from the state sector. Broackes was joined by

Victor (later Lord) Matthews, and Eric Parker as Finance Chief and now Chief Executive, and his team has made Trafalgar House a leading construction, engineering and shipping group, turning round many of these unglamorous acquisitions, expanding them by judicious investment, and thereby becoming one of the most consistently profitable stars of the stock market.

Trusthouse Forte employs 60,000 people across the world in a variety of activities centred around catering and hotels. Lord Forte, who began the company with a milk bar before the Second World War, remains Chairman of the Group and his son Rocco is Chief Executive. The Group now has over 200 hotels in the UK and Ireland, more than 550 in the USA and a scattering of luxury hotels across Europe and the rest of the world. Catering outlets include 200 Little Chef restaurants, motorway service areas and catering services to airlines, factories, offices and schools. Although the recession and a heavy programme of investment kept dividends and profits fairly flat during the early 1980s, THF is regarded as one of the most consistently profitable hotel groups in the world.

The **United Biscuits Group** employs over 40,000 people, 31,000 of whom are based in the UK. Formed from the amalgamation of a number of leading British food companies, its main activities are the manufacture and sale of food products through wholesale and retail outlets at home and abroad, under labels such as McVities, Crawfords, KP, Terry's and in the United States Keebler, and Spice Island Herbs.

Continued investment in new businesses has ensured rapid growth, with recent expansion into frozen food, restaurants and fast food. Turnover and profit have both nearly doubled in the past five years.

Introduction

This book has been written at a time of change, in the hope of influencing change. It unashamedly draws for its basic approach on the US book *In Search of Excellence*, but with major adaptations to take account of the very different industrial circumstances, practices and legislative environment in Britain, compared with the United States. The project was begun with an expectation that the characteristics that led to success among British companies would not necessarily be the same as those revealed by the American work – and that expectation has been fulfilled, sometimes in surprising ways.

British companies in the mid 1980s find themselves in strange circumstances. After years of being the poor man of industrial Europe, with low growth of gross national product (GNP) and a general atmosphere of industrial fatigue, suddenly they are emerging from the worst of the recession very much slimmer and fitter, with OECD sources predicting that Britain will race ahead in industrial growth. The regulatory environment has eased, as a result of government withdrawal from controls on pay, prices, dividends and foreign exchange. The spectre of trade union dominance of industrial relations, together with trade union influence on legislation, has dissipated to the extent that those managers who have the ability to manage, now also have the opportunity to do so. New organizational structures have been formed, which allow companies to be more flexible, quicker on their feet and environmentally aware – as they need to be to compete in international markets. At the same time, the domestic competition in many sectors is becoming fiercer, with the result that survivors are better equipped to tackle international markets.

To put all this down to political change would be naive. Even the present Government admits it can only help to create an environment which companies can take advantage of, and there are plenty of economists and other experts who will assure us that events are simply part of a natural cycle. What we are also witnessing is a social change within British companies, where the profit motive is being re-asserted with greater strength than has perhaps been the case since Victorian times and yet where the human values of work are also being strengthened – for those who have jobs, at least – as part of the realization that, in the end, productivity and profit come more from making the most of the people in an organization than from any other resource.

Amidst all this turmoil many companies have failed. Bankruptcies in early 1984 were still running at record levels, with few signs of the numbers easing up. Most companies battened down the hatches during the recession, cut numbers (often much later than they should have) and waited for better weather. Yet some companies stand out as having not merely ridden the storm, but having grown and found unexpected strengths while it lasted. These companies are often not in the sunrise industries, but in mature and even declining industries, such as shoes or raw materials. What gives these particular companies their *winning streak*?

We chose twenty-three companies which stood out from the crowd according to a number of success criteria, namely:

1. High growth in assets, turnover and profit over the past ten years (we allowed minor temporary dips for redirection). These companies expect to double or treble in size within a decade – and do.

2. A consistent reputation within the industrial sector as a leader. This is the company others imitate, or from which others try to poach talent. 'We are constantly under siege from headhunters,' says David Tagg, personnel director of a division of Grand Metropolitan, one of our twenty-three companies.

3. A solid public reputation. People generally feel good about this company and its operations.

We used several different routes to choose the companies that fulfilled all these criteria. One route was by plain and simple observation – some companies simply stand out in their industry. A second route was through detailed analysis by a small team of business school under-graduates, who sorted through the five- and ten-year results of dozens of companies. The third route was to gather the recommendations of the management consultancy division of the PA Group, whose consultants used their own intimate knowledge of British companies to evaluate them against our qualitative criteria. In order to ensure a balanced picture we limited the number of companies from any one segment of industry. We also excluded subsidiaries, except as part of a group, and the banks (both because of their peculiar financial structure and the fact that none of the big clearing banks stood out for the calibre of its management).

Interviews were carried out in all of these companies (with the sole exception of BTR, where we relied upon written materials), from chairman or managing director downwards, in many cases right down to the shop floor.

To the twenty-three who fulfilled all the criteria, we added another fifteen, each of whom met at least two of the criteria. These companies completed detailed questionnaires and provided internal documentation and other written materials. In some cases they also took part through in-depth interviews at top management level.

In addition to the advice and guidance from PA, our researches were aided by Peter Herbert of Henley – The Management College, whose own research for the Institute of Directors' Business Enterprise Award had already led him down many of the paths we needed to follow. Peter was able particularly to advise whether the success factors we identified applied equally to small business as to large. His own observations on success in small business are contained in Appendix 1, but suffice to say at this point that it is evident that the application of our overall results is relevant to businesses of any size.

A few examples, both from manufacturing and the service industries, will serve to illustrate just how strong the winning streak is in these successful companies. Racal, for example, has seen its assets grow from £15 million to £466 million between 1974 and 1983, while profits grew from £6 million to £114. Although this included two major takeovers in the UK alone, internal growth and profitability have been very high. One of those takeovers was in competition with the much more powerful and cash-rich GEC, also one of our successful companies. STC (Standard Telephones and Cables) has seen its share value rise fourfold since ITT sold its majority shareholding. Saatchi & Saatchi set itself the goal in the early 1970s, when it was a small and largely unknown operation, of joining the world leaders in the advertising agency business. By 1980 it was the largest in the UK; by 1981 it was the largest in Europe, and seventh in the world by 1983. It did this with an average compound growth rate of 31 per cent for twelve consecutive years. Its nearest competitors have grown at an average of 7 per cent compound during this time.

Of course, success or excellence does not have to be a permanent state of affairs. Companies can lose their winning streak if it is not assiduously maintained, and we recognized from the beginning that this could happen to a proportion of our sample over a period.

There is one further group of companies that we decided to include in our study, to overcome a perceived weakness in the American approach. Unsuccessful companies may also have common characteristics. Where these characteristics are shared with the successful companies, their value must be at least partially neutralized. On the other hand, where they are not shared with successful companies, there may be valuable clues as to management styles that should be avoided. In other words, could we match the characteristics of success with equivalent characteristics of failure? For this reason, we also chose a number of companies whose record against the success criteria was far from glorious. We attempted to identify the key characteristics of their management style from a mixture of interviews with past executives or with new management attempting to turn around a commercial loser, from literature searches and from comment by observers such as City analysts, management consultants and executive recruitment consultants.

So what's the point of the comparisons we shall be making in the coming chapters? Up till now, it has been difficult to be more precise about what makes for success in British companies other than to put it down to 'good ideas and good management'. In the following pages we shall attempt to isolate the characteristics of good management in successful British companies. We shall explore the attitudes and behaviour that these companies consistently demand and achieve from their managers and other employees, and how they do so. We shall seek to establish the set of standards by which each of these companies judges itself, which managers in companies without the winning streak can adopt and adapt to build their own sets of values, applicable to their company, in its industry and in its marketplace.

That is not to say that this is a book solely for top management. Far from it. *The Winning Streak* is aimed at everyone who has an interest in seeing our society function most efficiently to the greatest good of the greatest number. Being, in effect, an analysis of the capitalist enterprise at its best, the lessons learned here should be of value to anyone involved in the world of business and industry, from union official or business student to government minister, from ordinary employee to investment analyst and banker. To all of these audiences, whether they work in or with business, the results of our study should give a better understanding of how successful companies work and what they are like inside. Most importantly, they should provide a set of standards against which other enterprises can be judged.

In a book that draws its essence from comparisons, we cannot ignore comparisons that are inconvenient and embarrassing without weakening our argument as a whole. So it is essential to point out that success, or excellence as the American authors would prefer, is in itself a relative thing. While the United Kingdom admittedly exports three times more of its gross national product proportionately than the United States, there are only a few examples of British companies that are world beaters, compared with dozens from the United States. Numerous Japanese companies, too, have demonstrated in recent years that they have a stronger winning streak than British competitors. Success on the British stage alone is like starring in repertory in hopes of an invitation to London's West End or New York's Broadway.

If British companies are to perform among the stars on the world stage, they must transcend the attitudinal barriers that bind most organizations to the achievement of the acceptable in a small market tucked away in a corner of Europe. If British industry is to lead the national economic recovery (and no one else can do the job) then the winning streak will have to become endemic. Sir Ernest Harrison, chairman of Racal, insists that every one of the dozens of small companies that make up the electronics company should aim to become the best in the world in its field. If all British companies could set themselves the same objective, then the economic problems should take care of themselves.

1 Winning as a matter of style

After the first few interviews we began to wonder whether there were indeed any characteristics of management style common to all our sample of successful companies. Characteristics to which one company responded with instant recognition were equally strongly dismissed as insignificant by others. For example, companies such as Marks & Spencer or Clark's placed great stress on maintaining good relationships with suppliers, treating them almost as if they were customers. Yet other companies, such as Pritchard, saw supplier relations as of very minor interest.

The size and type of industry also seemed to affect the values that the different companies held dearest. The retailers in the sample, for example, were all enthusiastic believers in the virtues of centralized management, although they were very conscious of the importance of their outlets. Most other companies, however, espoused decentralization and profit-centre autonomy with equal fervour.

As we gathered more data, however, it became clear that there were indeed common characteristics of management style between the companies in the sample. What differed was the emphasis they placed on each of the characteristics and the way they interpreted them. These companies' ability to absorb and adapt management styles to their own circumstances – both the circumstances of marketplace and how mature their organization is – appeared crucial to their success stories.

It also became clear that organizational culture was a crucial element in the ability to maintain these characteristics consistently. So much so, in fact, that we found it more comfortable to talk about the commonalities between the companies not in terms of similar behaviours (especially when the different corporate cultures brought very different reactions to the same set of circumstances) but in terms of a broad perception or understanding in all the companies that certain issues *mattered*. These issues need not always be articulated; indeed it is a measure of their strength in many cases that they are evident but not remarked upon. 'That's simply the way we are' was a frequent comment from middle and junior management. The perception, the special way of looking at things, is so much a part of the company culture that it is an automatic director of everyday behaviour.

Before exploring what these common factors are, it is interesting to make some brief observations on the set of companies as a whole. One unexpected observation is that almost all are either family companies or strongly influenced by a founder. The first-generation companies include Trusthouse Forte (now rapidly becoming a second-generation family business with Rocco Forte as Chief Executive), Bejam, MFI, BTR and AGB; other companies, such as Clark's of Street, Bulmer, Plessey, Sainsbury and Marks & Spencer, are all family companies that have discovered the secret of maintaining growth and efficiency into several generations. How they do so is discussed in Chapter 10.

Another observation is the high proportion of companies whose interests are concentrated in mature industries such as rubber, shoes, construction, shipping or bricks. In some cases, though the industry as a whole is in decline, the particular company stands out against the trend. Clark's of Street, for example, has prospered while much of the rest of the British shoemaking industry has crumbled in the face of cheaper overseas imports.

By contrast, the number of very successful high-technology companies is relatively low. This perhaps reflects one of the principal problems of British industry.

Our sample also contains a relatively high proportion of retailers, reflecting the comparatively good performance of that sector in recent years. There are some arguments to suggest that the retail sector does not necessarily present a good example to follow, and we have borne these in mind in looking at retail companies. One particular argument says that retailers have gained their high profit performance by abusing their purchasing power to screw down manufacturers' margins and that this is a major cause of poor cash flow and lack of reinvestment in manufacturing. Retailers have forced manufacturers to adopt bar codes, for example, complains a director of a large consumer-product manufacturer. The codes add to manufacturing costs, while all the benefits go to the retailer, he maintains. Whether or not one accepts his argument, the large retailers have certainly not had to cope with fierce competition from overseas, as have so many manufacturers, so to some extent this is a sheltered industry.

Our sample also suggests that the day of the conglomerate is far from over. Hanson Trust, BTR, Trafalgar House and Grand Metropolitan are all diversified groups and all return very healthy profits.

The common characteristics we observed are as follows:

Leadership Demonstrated in a variety of ways, but particularly through visible top management, clear objectives at board level, and the creation of an environment where managers can lead. Top management in these companies accept that they have to be seen to be believed. The few shy and retiring chief executives are very visible to the key, senior employees who make the organization work – and they expect visible management from the managers in the front line. These top managers also have a clear sense, a vision, of where their company is going and communicate that vision down the line. They recognize that leadership at lower levels thrives where managers have and espouse understandable objectives and the resources and support to pursue them.

Autonomy Companies in different industries have different areas where they need to encourage entrepreneurial spirit. For the retailers it is among the buyers; for manufacturing and service industries it may be through independent small profit centres. Very successful companies with decentralized operations tend to have small bureaucracies, informal systems to keep units working together rather than against each other, a belief in the value of generalist managers, a positive attitude towards risk-taking, and to create an environment where managers are encouraged to take controlled initiative (i.e. where they have the freedom to manage in their own way within a clear framework of necessary restrictions).

Control Our successful companies all maintain very tight controls on areas that matter. They seek a balance between strict controls and the flexibility that all major businesses must have to react to market conditions and opportunities. Each has evolved its own solution to this innate conflict, but common factors include:

- tight limits on capital spending, combined with relative freedom to operate within agreed budgets

- close – in some cases almost fanatic – attention to business planning, combined with the ability to deal effectively with (and to expect) the unexpected
- constant feedback of results
- a long-term perspective – a clear understanding of where the company is going, and of its objectives, shared down the management hierarchy
- high standards that people are expected to adhere to

These companies tend to enforce the control perception by practice and by consensus that particular procedures are 'the right way of doing things' rather than by hefty rule books. Hence they are able to maintain a managerial approach that is regulated yet aggressive and opportunistic.

The involvement factor 'Everywhere else I've worked people have been cynical about the company. This is the first place I've found where people are positive about their employer,' says a middle manager at cleaning services company Pritchard. All the very successful companies in our survey appear to generate a remarkable level of commitment in their management levels, and most also manage to push that commitment down to the shop floor. Although the people they employ may not be exceptional, they extract from them extraordinary levels of performance.

Among the ingredients they use are:

- high pay and incentives
- stress on promotion from within
- creation of a *pride in ownership*, through equity participation, profit share schemes, or simply through a high level of consultation and discussion that makes people feel they have a real stake in the business
- stress on the importance of information, both what is needed just to do the job and provide feedback and what is needed to give people a broader understanding of the company and their role in it
- stress on training, both as a tool to increase efficiency and as a means of instilling the company's values into all employees
- recognition of the importance of the 'social' side of work. Many of our sample either spend considerable effort on making the working environment enjoyable or, in some cases, create a substantial off-duty social life, or both

These companies are not afraid of being labelled paternalistic. Indeed they see their behaviour towards employees as both enlightened self-interest and a necessary part of an efficient organization.

Market orientation Successful companies understand and inter-react closely with their market. The brand image is important to them, especially if it is tied closely to the company identity, as is St Michael to Marks & Spencer, or Clark's to shoes. That 'the customer is king' is axiomatic in their operations. Every function of the company has as its prime objective the satisfaction of customer requirements. To establish those customer requirements, they go to great lengths to gather detailed market information. Quality control is intrinsic in everything they do.

Zero basing (keeping in close touch with the fundamentals of the business) Successful companies either never get away from the basic principles of the business or, if they do, are quick to revert to them. These companies habitually take an introspective look at what they are doing and why, and relate this to their core objectives. The perception can almost be summed up by what is said to be the family motto of shoemakers Clark's: 'But will it sell shoes?'

All of our companies have stuck closely to their last. This includes the conglomerates such as Hanson Trust and BTR, which have chosen specific types of industry and stuck with them. Where any of our sample companies have ventured away from their last – as Bejam did into fast-food restaurants – it has usually been a failure. However, the companies have always recognized their mistakes and withdrawn rapidly.

Staying with the fundamentals often requires careful attention to detail, and some of our sample are almost obsessive on this score. 'Retail is detail' say the Sainsburys.

The innovation factor These companies have a continuous interest and commitment to things new, to the process of change. They may, like Sainsbury, actively help along social change. They are among the leaders in bringing new concepts to the market, especially where technology is concerned.

The internal barriers to change are much lower in our successful companies than in British industry in general. This is as much a matter of management style as organizational structure – managerial confidence that things can be done, that the individual's job is not at risk, helps the process along. The way the organization itself develops in response to change varies greatly between firms, but is consistent within the individual firm's culture. Most of these companies exhibit a natural curiosity about how things are done elsewhere; they tend to have an international perspective even if their market is narrowly focused on the UK.

They see innovation not as an end in itself, but as a means to the primary objective of making ever greater profits by satisfying the customer. Hence research and development tend to be heavily – if not wholly – market directed.

The integrity perception Our companies have built integrity into their way of doing business, to the extent that it is not out of place to talk of a 'passion for integrity'. It applies equally to employees, to customers, to suppliers and to other audiences such as the community.

Insofar as employees are concerned, it is largely a matter of ensuring that people know where they stand and that they are being dealt with fairly.

The same applies to the customer and the supplier. The customer receives high quality of goods and service, value for money, swift and effective handling of complaints and the information he needs about the company's products. Suppliers like to deal with these companies – even where they drive a hard bargain on price – because they are reliable. Relationships between these companies and their suppliers are often highly developed, especially in the generation of new products to fit market needs.

Most of these companies would be very shaken by any bad press that attacked their integrity. They expend considerable effort in the maintenance of a public image as good corporate citizens.

The common element of all these items is that most of them seem very obvious. They seem common sense, and not unduly complex. Yet it is quite clear that the typical British company either ignores or minimizes the importance of some or (in all too many cases) all of them. While most companies may, for example, espouse high standards in the annual report, the message does not appear to penetrate to the troops. These relatively simple perceptions turn out to be very difficult to apply – and it becomes more difficult, the more complex the business is.

In the following chapters, we take each of these items and attempt to

11

show how they are perceived by the very successful companies, and what that means in terms of management practice in those organizations. If there is one lesson that emerges from this analysis of best practice in British enterprise it is that success appears to stem from doing a lot of fairly simple and obvious things well.

2 Leadership

'Success is about leadership and leadership is about success' –
Sir Michael Edwardes

What makes a leader? Few of the most successful companies make a song and dance about leadership, yet in all of them managers down the line pinpoint effective leadership at chairman or chief executive level as a key to their own motivation and the company's success. In many cases they refer to the chief executive's charisma.

Whether the chief executive has charisma or not, line managers have confidence both that the top management team knows where it is going and that they should follow. Says one manager at United Biscuits: 'If Sir Hector [Laing] says he is going to do something, we will follow. Then we'll begin to ask questions twenty-four hours later.'

'His personal example, the hours he works, his care for people, convince the employees he is rooting night and day for the business,' adds Robert Clark, chief executive of United Biscuits UK.

The perception of leadership in most of these companies comprises three elements, upon which others may be built. These elements are:

- that leaders are visible
- that leaders provide a clear mission, which they believe in passionately themselves and incite others to subscribe to
- that leadership thrives where people have clear objectives and the resources to strike out after them

Leaders are visible

'Leadership here is all about talking to people,' says STC's Sir Kenneth Corfield. It is a message he puts into practice and expects others in the company to follow. Touring round the units, discussing where and how the business is going, is an integral part of every senior manager's routine.

The same message comes equally strongly from the chairmen and executives of Trusthouse Forte, Sainsbury, Marks & Spencer and a host of other successful companies – employee confidence that top management knows what it is doing comes best from face-to-face encounters. Sir Hector Laing, chairman of United Biscuits, travels round with a jug of orange juice which he uses at the slightest excuse to demonstrate how the company value-added cake is divided up between employees, re-investment, dividends and interest, and tax. Sir John Sainsbury keeps an annual log of all his site visits and compares year to year to ensure that he always visits at least one hundred. These visits are not mere formalities. They are designed to keep him closely in touch with the grass roots of the business.

Lord Sieff, until he retired in 1984, was to be seen in the M&S stores more than anywhere else. 'He commands great respect wherever he goes,' commented one M&S manager. On one occasion near to retirement, when very heavy snowfalls had blocked most main roads, he still insisted on driving from London all the way down to Chatham, just to thank the sales assistants for turning up in spite of the weather. A telephone call would have sufficed to pass on the content of the message but the only way to put across the genuine appreciation that top management felt was to go there and tell people in person.

Sieff's weekly routine included telephone calls every Saturday at around five p.m. to four or five stores chosen at random, to check on how the day's trading had gone. To the branch managers contacted in this way without warning it was a valuable reminder that top management really was interested in their progress.

The philosophy that real understanding of the business only comes from constant exposure to the sharp end – where it meets the customer – goes all the way down the Marks & Spencer management tree. Every one of the 260 stores in Britain is visited by at least one director a year. All headquarters executives spend a high proportion of their time in the stores and once every eighteen months or so they spend an entire week sitting alongside a branch manager as he does his job. 'He works alongside the manager and talks to everyone. You learn a lot. You don't know how much paperwork the manager has to deal with, for example, until you sit with him at his desk on a Tuesday morning.'

At Trusthouse Forte, Lord Forte established a similar pattern of regular site visits. 'Keeping track of the grass roots is an essential part of the way this company works,' explains his son Rocco, now chief executive, who has automatically adopted the same approach. 'The more people at the centre sit back and let one person tell them about each area, the less in touch they are. I walk into an hotel and I can see straight away how it is being kept. It makes me aware of problems long before they appear in the figures.'

In the same way Sir Lawrie Barratt spends at least five days a month on site across his housebuilding empire. 'You quickly get the feel of whether the people there are pulling together as a team,' he explains.

When Derek Hunt of MFI wants to get an important new message across to staff, he does so in person, hiring conference centres around the country to explain why what he wants them to do is important. For example, in June 1983 the company conducted a major review of every aspect of its operations where they touched the customer, from letters, through the warehouseman's way of addressing people to advertising and distribution. 'I spoke to every single one of the 3500 staff. The response was dramatic,' he declares. One result was that the quality control department began to lean more heavily on buyers and suppliers, while the expectations of the sales staff were raised so that they, too, reacted whenever they found a below-standard product.

The regular presence of top management on site is accepted as normal by the employees. When asked the main difference between MFI and previous employers, one manager remarked: 'I never once saw the managing director of British Homes Stores when I worked there; here I am on first-name terms with the MD.'

Bill Perry, joint managing director of frozen-food retail chain Bejam, tours his branches constantly. 'There is very little formality,' he says. 'We get people together at all levels during these visits for brain-stormings. I often sit down with the branch manager and we take the company to pieces and put it back together again. These visits are important because they make people feel you are taking care of their jobs.'

'Perry spends hours talking with branch managers about their ideas,' says finance director John Edwards.

Allied Breweries managing director Douglas Strachan makes a habit, when visiting depots, of walking up to the first person he sees and introducing himself. It takes many employees by surprise, and many of them can be forgiven for an initial suspicion that they are the victim of a practical joke, but the internal public relations value is considerable.

Brian Nelson, group managing director of cidermakers Bulmer, is not a household name. Yet every one of the company's 1800 workers knows him well. Nelson makes a habit of being seen on the shop floor. He also spends a day every six months or so working alongside the delivery crews as a lorry driver's mate. He does not do so from any desire to be one of the boys, but rather from the practical point of view that it gives him the opportunity to observe working practices at first hand and gives the employees a chance to talk to him much more frankly than would be possible in the more formal atmosphere of his office.

These excursions provide a bonus since he can listen to customer comments and complaints in a manner that would not normally be afforded to a senior executive.

The drivers do not resent Nelson's presence. On the contrary, they rather enjoy being able to deflect complaints with, 'No need to tell me. Tell my mate over there – he's the managing director.'

An indication of how well they appreciate the interest of senior management in what they do, and of the rapport that can be built up between the shop floor and the executive suite, is the employee reaction to mistakes that the executives make in the unfamiliar working environment. On one excursion with a delivery lorry, Nelson opened the cab window. To his horror, all the delivery notes blew straight out of the window on to the motorway.

Pulling into the nearest service area, the driver shook his head when Nelson suggested he telphone back to headquarters for new instructions. 'You did it. You call,' he insisted. Recognizing the justice of the comment, Nelson did so. On return to the depot, Nelson was confronted with a delegation from the other drivers. Their object? To present him with a clipboard so it wouldn't happen again.

Executives at C. & J. Clark receive the same camaraderie from shop-floor employees. The company mythology abounds with tales of how directors have mucked in to help out with one crisis or another. 'One winter when it was difficult to get the product out in time, management became a second shift,' recalls John Clothier, managing director of Clark's retailing division. 'The unions accepted it because they had all the overtime they wanted and they understood why it was necessary. They still pull my leg about the mistakes I made packing boxes on to the trucks. The same happens when I take a spell in the retail shops, if I sell some shoes and forget to try to sell the customer some polish as well.'

At Racal, Sir Ernest Harrison delights in leading from the front. 'He always tries to lead by setting an example,' comments a veteran manager in the company. 'If an urgent delivery has to be got out he will ask the factory manager what he can do. He will make the tea or knock nails into packing cases if asked to. He tries to get all the younger managers to set the same example.' Most of them do.

All of these illustrations reinforce the research conducted over the past decade in the United States by Dr Richard Ruch of the School of Business at Ryder College, New Jersey. Ruch started with a vast opinion survey of 5000 General Motors employees, and tried to analyse what the factors were that most affected productivity. One block of questions covered how employees viewed their immediate supervisor and the company's top management.

It turned out that the employees' perception of top management was far more significant in terms of job satisfaction and general motivation than their perception of the supervisor. The supervisor was able for the most part only to help or hinder them in the practical accomplishment of their jobs. To top management, however, they looked for reassurance that they were valued as individuals, and that their welfare was more important than figures on a balance sheet.

Ruch found that, even where GM had invested considerable effort in upgrading employee/supervisor relationships at the shop-floor level, the benefits could easily be cancelled out if the employees held a negative opinion of top management. A negative view of top management correlated highly with poor records of attendance, labour turnover and industrial accidents, while a positive view showed the opposite effect. Ruch also detected a correlation between incidence of mental illness and negative attitudes towards top management.

Ruch continued his work with a unit of AT&T and was subsequently able to explain employees' perceptions of their superiors in these terms:

Employees directly associate the following with supervisory management: treating workers with respect as individuals; clearly explaining appraisal standards; providing information needed to do the job properly; and equitable treatment.

On the other hand, employees tend to associate the following with top management:

- informing employees ahead of time about changes that will affect their jobs;
- caring about how employees really feel about their work, being open and honest in dealing with employees;
- giving serious consideration to employee suggestions;
- giving supervisors enough authority to get the job done;
- making a strong commitment to serving the customer;

- having the ability to solve major company problems;
- running a socially responsible organization;
- providing new services and products required to meet competition;
- placing more emphasis on the *quality* than the *quantity* of work.

Now the strength of negative attitudes towards top management depends to a large extent on just how visible the directors are. It is much easier to curse and blame a distant, faceless 'them' than a tangible human being. Top management does not have to be *liked* – although it helps – but to extract the best out of people it does have to be *respected* and *trusted*. 'If a leader is never seen, how can he be trusted?' asks Sir Hector Laing pointedly.

When we talk here about top-management image, it does not necessarily have to mean how people see the group chairman. The key is in who people see themselves working for. While employees of Trusthouse Forte by and large still see themselves working for Lord Forte, or at least for the Forte family, few employees of the Hanson Trust, by contrast, have ever encountered Lord Hanson himself or would expect to. The reason is that the Hanson Trust has a clear policy of encouraging employees to identify with the operating company they work for, rather than a distant holding company. Says Hanson: 'It's counterproductive for me to appear in the factories. Employees of Ever Ready know that it is Ron Fulford who turned their company round, not me.'

Peter Harper, like every other subsidiary chairman in Hanson Trust, takes on the same role of top-management visibility in his company, the UDS Group (now renamed Allders), as the chairmen of the large integrated companies such as Sainsbury do in theirs. 'The important thing is to be seen,' he stresses. 'I went to a late-night sale in a Glasgow store within the first few weeks. It was the first time they had ever seen a director at one of those events.' Harper's colleague Dick Garrett, chairman of Northern Amalgamated Industries, spreads open his diary to demonstrate that he only has three days in his office in the next five weeks – the rest of his time is on the road, making personal visits to the collection of small companies that he is responsible for.

The very knowledge that the chairman will be visiting helps to keep the operational units on their toes, especially when there is a serious problem. Harper recalls when he took over the chairmanship of UDS: 'In my first ten days I discovered that an Australian subsidiary was posting a loss for the quarter. I telexed and flew out. By the time I arrived the managers had planned what they were going to do and started to implement it. All I did was make them speed it up a little.' The jolt given to the unit's complacency galvanized management all the way down the line. As Harper toured the outposts he found that the smallest and most obscure depot had pinned up on its wall the message that 'the name of the game is profitability'.

Whether the visible leadership should come from the very top or not is basically a matter of both corporate organization and corporate culture, both of which of course are closely intertwined. The successful company establishes at which level visible leadership is most appropriate and makes sure that the executives at that level are seen to be seen. In some cases, this means that group chairmen who do carry charisma bite their tongues and stay out of the limelight. For example, Lord Hanson rarely attends functions in the operating companies, for fear of undermining the image of the subsidiary chairman as the man in charge. On the rare occasions when he does make his presence felt in the operating companies, it is in response to a particular need, such as parent company reassurance to a sales force after a necessary but unpleasant removal of a senior sales executive. On that occasion, recalls Harper, 'Hanson spoke for about an hour. At the end, one of the salesmen told me: "I didn't understand a word, but that was great!"'

Daniel Clark also prefers that the employees identify with the unit managers for business leadership. Although he is more than prepared to muck in, explains a middle manager, 'All the hand-shaking and visible leadership is delegated to the people with immediate profit responsibility. Half the factory workers wouldn't recognize Daniel Clark if he walked round their workshop.'

Perhaps the least visible chief executive of our sample is Lord Weinstock, who scarcely ever visits the plants. Weinstock's presence, however, is felt everywhere in GEC. He is, as any GEC manager who brings in poor results knows only too well, only a telephone call away. 'The old man' exerts a highly individual brand of leadership. Down below, however, the managers in the field are expected to lead in a more conventional manner – though how they do so is less important than whether they deliver the profit levels expected of them.

'Leadership for me is a one-on-one affair,' Weinstock explains; it is best exerted in personal meetings where people can discuss issues without the need to pose for an audience. And he strongly defends his practice of keeping out of the plants.

'When I had two factories, I knew all the girls there,' he recalls. 'Every

19

fortnight I'd spend two or three days in the factory. Not making tours of inspection, having the troops drawn up in full ceremonial. The purpose was to make sure people did things better.

'Now, with between 300 and 400 factories, I can't do that. If I spent two hours in every plant each year, I'd never come into this office at all. Anyway, if the chief executive arrives on an arranged visit, people show him what they want him to see. If they say let's turn right, I say, "No, left." I stop and talk to the operators, so it's not a great success from their point of view. And I suspect that the next day they are doing precisely the same as they were before I came.'

When these executives do turn up on site, however, they tend to be highly discreet. Sir Maxwell Joseph once turned up to a new Grand Metropolitan restaurant and asked for a table, only to be refused because he had not made a reservation. Joseph left without demur and only later did the restaurant staff learn who they had turned away. The fact that it was accepted they had done their job, and that it was appreciated rather than resented at top-management level, travelled round the company along with the chortles at the *faux pas*. Much the same happened when Associated Dairies chairman Noel Stockdale tried to pay by cheque for his goods at an Asda store. The check-out assistant refused, on the ground that the cheque was above the value she was allowed to accept.

Leaders provide a clear mission

In discussing the nature of leadership with middle and junior managers in our successful companies, time and again it emerged that they accepted that the top-management team knew where they were taking the company and why. By contrast, as we shall see in Chapter 11, in unsuccessful companies there is frequently massive confusion about top management's long-term objectives. In the successful companies when the board says, 'This is where we intend to be in five years' time,' managers down the line believe it and set about trying to make it happen. In unsuccessful companies managers nod politely, agree among themselves that there will be another change in direction before too long and concentrate on the short-term objectives, which experience has shown them top management really wants.

This sense of mission is particularly noticeable in successful family companies, where the founder's original objectives have often been reinforced over generations. As long as those objectives remain relevant, they provide a natural framework for everyone in the company to work with. This framework has been adequate to steer the group through major strategic changes, rather than box it into a set and increasingly obsolete mould.

The broad group objectives at Sainsbury probably do not need to be written down, because they are so much a part of the company culture. For younger companies such as Saatchi & Saatchi, however, the written statement of objectives is an important part of creating and reinforcing the culture they wish to evolve. It is significant that many of the successful companies in our survey have painstakingly developed broad statements of purpose that enable staff at all levels to understand what their company wants to be.

These statements of mission may often sound trite, but the reality is that top management believes in them and convinces people lower down the hierarchy that they do. Three of these statements are reproduced in Appendix 3. Among the statements worthy of note are those from Saatchi and from STC. Saatchi's detailed statement of principles has appeared in its annual reports year after year almost unchanged. It provides a relatively detailed explanation of top management's concept of business development as regards employees, clients, organization, creativity, market position, finance, productivity and product superiority.

'It's a clear philosophy, clearly articulated,' says Maurice Saatchi. 'It's being consistent that counts. In every new business presentation we give to clients, we do so on the basis that this is our credo. People indoctrinate themselves. Our observation of our clients is that the most successful ones also have a very clear business philosophy.'

STC also sets out its philosophy in an unequivocal way. To a certain extent the small booklet that every employee receives, 'The Best Company Book', is a reflection of the cultural imperatives of a company which for all but its most recent history has been a minor outpost of a highly disciplined US multinational. Instead of being a summary of top management's view of the company's broad objectives, however, it is primarily a reflection of how the mass of employees view what their company should stand for – which is perhaps a more accurate reflection of corporate culture than could ever be put down by even the chief executive himself.

The origins of the document go back to the mid 1970s when, says STC

21

director Neville Cooper, 'We were getting a bit complacent. The chairman sprang on us that we should aim to be the best company in the UK. There was some dissension at first, and a few cries of "ridiculous", then after further discussion we all agreed it was better to have a really tough goal to aim at.

'We set up a lot of committees all round the company, including shop-floor people, and asked them: "What does it mean to you to be the best company?" The answer came back clearly:

– to be efficient, profitable and give good service to our customers
– to do business straight and honestly
– to treat all employees with respect and to help them develop and contribute fully
– to have an open and participative style of management.'

These objectives, broad as they are, have formed the basis of most policy decisions taken in the company ever since then. The involvement of so many people in crystallizing the objectives has meant that the level of commitment to them down the line is high.

To these very broad statements of intent are added more specific financial and market goals based on long-term planning. For example, STC aims to triple sales turnover this decade. The goal is not simply a growth target for its own sake, but is closely tied to the company statement of philosophy. 'We reckon that one of our duties is to try to maintain the level of employment, now about 30,000 people,' says Cooper. 'The only way we can do that while constantly improving productivity is to generate massive increases in sales.'

AGB has set itself a series of general goals for expansion over the rest of the decade. The company aims to derive 40 per cent of its income from information systems activities by 1990 and to increase its penetration of Far East markets.

'I have to keep testing our vision and constantly updating it,' says AGB chairman Bernard Audley. 'We hold executive seminars involving about 200 of our key people to monitor and also to refine – or re-define – the vision. Since this involves assembling the top staff from twenty different countries we restrict ourselves to one such mega-session every other year. It is immensely valuable to all concerned. At the first such seminar in 1978 I said that our turnover would be up from £7 million to £50 million with profits of £5 million and that we would achieve this not solely from market research but on a broadened base, for example in publishing, marketing services and information systems. This provoked not a little scepticism at the time and fears of a new era of "management by surprise".'

Surprise or not, having provided a target which assumed a 40 per cent per annum compound growth over the next six years Audley set the managers to discussing how they would go about achieving it. The more they discussed it, the more opportunities they saw. By the end of the meeting there was a consensus that it could be done and everyone was committed to ensuring that it *was* done. In the event, the compound growth per annum by 1984 was not 40 per cent but 50 per cent. 'Of all the events I participate in, this is the one that gives me the most charge,' says Audley. 'You can feel the power under the roof. There is totally open discussion and no holds barred, at the main session and at the separate group sessions. If I'm shown to be on a hobby horse, I can be required to dismount. But once someone has assented I am going to ask him to do it.'

In all of the successful companies, the chief executive spends a major proportion of his time making sure that the message of the corporate mission and goals comes across. BOC's group chief executive Dick Giordano believes that the chief executive 'is in large measure a teacher or proselytizer. He can push four or five principles in his dealings with managers – for example, increasing shareholder wealth, developing managers, being good citizens and building durable customer bases – and he has to do so constantly.'

'You have to keep telling people your values,' says Douglas Strachan, managing director of Allied-Lyons' beer division. 'If you repeat it often enough, it does get down the line.'

At Trusthouse Forte, Rocco Forte encapsulates the company's attitude towards leadership in this way: 'Leadership draws people in. It gives them an overall philosophy, outlook and commitment. There's an element of nagging persistence in keeping on top of things that need it.'

And that, of course, brings us full circle back to visible management, because in spite of the advances in communications technology, there is still no better way to inculcate these special values and goals than by telling them in person.

Clear objectives – the environment where all managers can lead

Precise objectives and limits of authority at the operating level give middle and junior managers the means to lead within the overall framework. Says John Clothier of Clark's retail division: 'The core value of our business is clear lines of responsibility. Can someone say: "I did that!"?'

At Clark's, all managers down to foreman level are instilled with the understanding that what counts is return on assets employed, and that their performance will be judged primarily against that criterion. The limits of authority are very clearly defined. Says PA consultant Mike Barnes: 'Clark's is almost military in its attitude to leadership. Those who prove they can handle people become line officers; the others are given staff positions.'

At Bulmer, says Nelson, 'Leadership has to be against a base where people are free to act. They must be able to see the results of their decisions. Sometimes a manager or foreman wants to hold things to himself. But we insist that he provides accurate definitions of responsibility for his subordinates just as he has been given clear guidelines himself. In this way, we can push responsibility down as far as possible.'

'Leadership', echoes BOC's Giordano, 'should not be embodied in any single person. When you are spread out as we are, you need lots of leaders. Leadership has to be combined with knowledge and the right set of goals.'

A major part of creating the environment where people down the hierarchy can take this kind of leadership is the attention that many of our successful companies pay to developing leaders. At Bulmer, the recognition of good leadership as part of the success recipe is so much part of the organizational culture that it has spawned its own school of leadership, based on 'outward bound' principles. 'We started with team-building exercises where people do things they have never done before. The leadership of the team rotates so that everyone gets a turn and is criticized by the other team members. It changed people's attitudes so well we formed the Leadership Trust, which is now an independent organization.'

Bulmer's concept of leadership extends beyond management to the unions, too, on the principle that an effective union representative respected by his members is much easier to deal with than an ineffective one.

Other companies attempt to instil leadership early in young managers by throwing them in at the deep end. STC often gives young managers their head in taking an idea to its logical conclusion as a new venture. Usually this involves a product that fits closely into the general development strategy, but on occasions young managers are allowed to develop ideas with little or no relevance to the core business, simply to expose them to practical experience of leadership in a start-up situation. Explains Corfield: 'We give funding for ventures the company has no great interest in, where it will develop the ability of entrepreneurial managers. For example, one small group of young men found we had an unused asset in two large tanks where submarine cable had been stored underwater, before that activity was transferred elsewhere. They also discovered that we had an underground tributary of the Thames flowing through the site, which we could tap. They proposed a fish farm, whose production went to London for smoking. The venture ran for several years before the water deteriorated and it had to be closed down.

'It was a near success, but the important thing was it gave them a good grounding in leadership. There was no loss of prestige for them when they themselves decided it was not worth further investment.'

A similar opportunity occured when STC's Newport plant suffered a drought and had to drill a well. 'They came to the board and asked if they could set up a bottling plant for STC mineral water,' says Corfield. Given the go-ahead, they found out the hard way that the mineral water market was a tough and competitive business. Eventually they found a market for the product in the pharmaceutical industry where its special properties, including low ionization, made it an ideal medical solvent. The business is now worth £2 million a year.

'These', says Corfield, 'are the type of people who tend to get promoted in our company.'

Clark's, too, believes strongly in developing leadership abilities as fast as possible. Young graduate recruits to the retailing side are likely to find themselves running a shop within six months. 'It means they can't back off from dealing with problems,' explains a training manager. 'It puts pressure on them very quickly. But very few sink. We keep half of them for more than five years. If they stay that long they usually stay for good.'

Pritchard frequently places managers into make or break environments. The two young managers appointed to run a local authority contract for parks and open spaces in Wandsworth wondered what had hit them when they found themselves embroiled in a political strike that made national headlines. They coped extremely well, says Pritchard. They talked with the strikers, organized the continuation of the work and sweet-talked the local council. What made them able to cope, and brought out the leadership qualities in them, was the fact that they had both delegated authority and unequivocal support from the management levels above. Senior managers demonstrated that support by turning up to join in cutting the grass themselves.

Also important to the environment where leadership can flourish is accountability, described by Pritchard's finance director David Openshaw as the characteristic on which chairman Peter Pritchard places greatest stress. Everyone in the organization knows exactly what his role is and what his objectives are, even in staff functions. This accent on personal accountability is echoed in every one of our successful companies. Leadership, in these companies, involves being allowed to make mistakes; it results in positive attitudes towards problem solving, by making people accountable for solutions rather than just for the problem.

Colin Marshall, chief executive of British Airways, a company emerging from a lengthy period of poor results, has this to say of the kind of management he is trying to create to turn the company round:

'Making mistakes is acceptable. Indeed, if they are not making mistakes, they are probably conserving rather than managing. Furthermore they will be judged on the speed and efficiency of the repairs, not the mere ratio of hits and misses. Of course, they must learn from such mistakes.'

Each of the successful companies has its own conception of the perfect leader in its environment, tailored to fit the lessons of its own culture. However, few if any would dispute Sir Kenneth Corfield's definition that it is someone 'with the ability to unleash the aspirations of people who work for him'. But probably the prize for the most detailed definition of leadership must go to Daniel Clark, who says: 'The leader at junior- or middle-management level must have a clear idea of corporate objectives, know what's going on around him, be sensitive to both bosses and subordinates, logical, consistent and persistent, know when to smile and when to frown – and above all he needs to be a human being.'

Practice versus theory

How does all this fit the accepted wisdom on leadership?

The qualities which make a leader have been explored in depth by a variety of academics and consultants, notably John Adair in Britain and Professor Abraham Zaleznik in the United States. Zaleznik, who teaches at Harvard's Graduate School of Business, differentiates strongly between leadership and management. The two roles are, he believes, very different and require very different people. The effective manager is essentially someone who motivates other people and administers resources to ensure that the company's objectives are fulfilled. The effective leader motivates people to create and follow new objectives.

Zaleznik describes the typical leader as 'active rather than reactive, shaping ideas rather than responding to them'. Leaders adopt a personal and active attitude towards goals. By contrast, 'managerial practice focuses on the decision-making process rather than ultimate events. . . . Where managers act to limit choices, leaders work in the opposite direction, to develop fresh approaches to long-standing problems and to open issues for new options.'

Zaleznik's analysis of leadership leads him to several interesting conclusions. Firstly, he finds that 'a leader is more interested in what events and decisions mean to people than in his own role in getting things accomplished'. Leaders are often viewed by others with strong emotions. 'Leaders attract strong feelings of identity and difference, or of love and hate. Human relations in leader-dominated structures often appear turbulent, intense, and at times even disorganized. Such an atmosphere intensifies individual motivation and often produces unanticipated outcomes.'

Managers on the other hand are much more rational in their approach. They want to be liked and avoid solutions that might cause confrontation. 'They focus subordinates' attention on procedures rather than on the substance of decisions, communicate in signals rather than clearly stated messages, and play for time to take the sting out of win–lose situations.'

Secondly, he finds that 'Leaders tend to feel somewhat apart from their environment and other people. . . . It is this separate sense of self that makes leaders agents of change, whether technological, political or ideological.' The typical manager, however, needs to feel that he belongs to a team, that he is fulfilling a clear and useful role within the organization.

Finally, he observes that the leaders who motivate the most significant changes may not be those with the greatest dash and verve. Charisma, though it is a frequent companion of leadership, is not an essential ingredient, and can all too easily lead people astray. This point is rein-forced admirably in Alistair Mant's *tour de force, The Leaders We Deserve.* Mant demonstrates that the best leaders are often not the most aggressive, that the hard guy with the drive all too often doesn't know where he is driving to. The quieter, persistent leader, who has a broader vision and understanding, is more likely to lead people in profitable directions.

John Adair also draws a distinction between autocracy and leader-ship. People will follow the autocrat during times of crisis, but will resent and resist him at other times. Adair sees the leader as having four key skills – influence, persuasion, guidance and support – which he applies by adapting his management style to different situations. Adair also asserts that the leader has three major functions, achieving the task, motivating the group and motivating the individual.

Adair's ideas tend to apply best to the manager at the operating level, rather than the visionary at the top. Accepting that distinction, the prac-tice in our successful companies does seem to equate well with both theories. The chief executive in most of these companies provides the long-term vision, the challenge to established routines and the sense of knowing where the company is going that characterizes Zaleznik's description of leadership. At the same time, the environment down the line is such that managers there are free to develop and demonstrate leadership in Adair's sense of the word.

A major factor in creating that environment is the degree and nature of the autonomy granted to operating units. And that is the subject of the next chapter.

3 Autonomy

'I don't mind what they do as long as it turns out all right' –
Lord Weinstock of GEC

The relationship between company culture and company structure is complex and largely unexplored. That each influences the other is clear, but how they do so is still pretty much a mystery.

In our sample of companies we have, with minor exceptions, two camps. At the one extreme are the decentralists, who operate as federations of independent small units. At the other end are the centralists, who have large functional departments at headquarters and very limited autonomy at operating level. With one exception, the centralists are all retailers; we have so far not been able to find an example of a highly successful British manufacturing company with a heavily centralized organization.

One possible conclusion from this is that retailers are a case apart, operating in a distinctive environment where the natural laws of business efficiency are reversed. But we believe the answer lies elsewhere. In their book, *In Search of Excellence*, American authors Peters and Waterman observed that successful companies had the maximum of autonomy, except in certain key areas, which top management held to be so important that they had to retain a central rein on them. This observation holds generally true for our sample of successful British companies. The difference between the retailers and other organizations is that the retailers feel there are more areas that need a guiding hand from the centre. The maintenance of margins, for example, is heavily dependent upon central buying.

'We are selling consistency,' says Sir John Sainsbury. 'The customer has to feel familiar with the layout and goods offered in any of our stores, wherever they are in the country.' The whole sales pitch is based on the customer's knowledge that the packet of frozen peas he buys in Lancashire will be the same quality and value for money wherever he goes within that shopping chain. So the key areas where the retailers maintain central control include design, presentation, stock and pricing, as well as more commonplace areas such as capital expenditure. Significantly, the less successful retailers have had the greatest autonomy at shop level in these areas.

Where the successful retailers do allow considerable autonomy is in the organization and motivation of the people within the stores. This, says John Clothier of Clark's retail division, is where the real difference comes in returns from stores of comparable size and location. A really good manager can increase sales by up to 30 per cent, he believes, simply by how effectively he uses his people.

Lord Sieff, whose company exerts rather more direct controls on the individual store manager, puts the difference between the good and bad store manager at 10 per cent above or below average. On individual store turnovers of millions of pounds that difference affects the bottom line considerably.

The other strongly centralized company in our sample is Trusthouse Forte. 'Central control has made this business what it is,' declares Rocco Forte. There is considerable delegation of control to the divisions, to take account of the different product areas. But within, say, the hotel division, the areas of responsibility delegated to the individual hotel manager are severely constrained. Decisions on pricing, advertising, décor and capital investment all tend to be taken at divisional headquarters. 'Our business is all about maintaining standards,' says Lord Forte. 'Unless you have direct control, that's very hard.'

'Where the THF hotel manager has a lot of autonomy is going out and getting business,' says Rocco. 'He has a budget, which he is involved in preparing, and which sets a staff standard and parameters on gross margins, operating profits, maintenance expenditure and so on. But he has no direct authority on development or refurbishment of the property. Every hotel manager is happier if he has new rooms and a new restaurant. But you can spend a lot of money on these things ineffectually.'

That there can be autonomy in a centralized organization is born out by THF's experience in Paris, when it acquired the three grand hotels, the George V, La Tremoille and the Plaza-Athenée.

The unions of the three hotels had campaigned vociferously against a foreign takeover, parading in their chef, bellboy and waiter uniforms outside the hotels to attract public attention. Having won control, Forte discovered that management in the Plaza-Athenée had effectively abdicated, leaving the day-to-day running of the business to the union. In one of those flashes of insight that distinguish the entrepreneurial genius from the normal businessman, Forte offered the post of managing director to the shop steward, who happened to be chief concierge.

The choice was not as irrational as it might have appeared. In analysing the problems of the hotel, it quickly became clear to the THF representative in Paris that the head concierge had a clearer idea than anyone else of what needed to be done.

The new managing director introduced a regime of remarkable employee participation, quite unlike anything found elsewhere in THF. An employee consultative committee took over the handling of lateness, absenteeism and other disciplinary matters. An incentive scheme was worked out under which the employees shared with THF all profits above 5 per cent of turnover. In return, the labour force was reduced by 20 per cent. Profits rose dramatically to three and a half times the level on acquisition. The remaining employees saw their annual income double over a five-year period.

The experience in Paris gradually fed into THF hotels in Britain and made a significant contribution to productivity across the group.

For the decentralized companies, several common factors emerge, among them:

- they have small headquarters bureaucracies
- they maintain the business as much as possible in small units, each with its own clear mission, tied into overall organizational goals
- they have relatively informal systems of ensuring that the independent units work with rather than against each other, while at the same time keeping inter-trade on a strictly commercial basis
- they have action-oriented, informal management teams
- they have a positive attitude towards risk-taking

Small headquarters bureaucracies

None of these companies has an imposing or palatial headquarters building stuffed with hundreds of scurrying staff. Indeed, the average is about forty, with an upper limit of about one hundred and sixty, and a lower limit of as little as twenty. In the operating subsidiaries, even though they have many more functions, it is often even fewer. For example, GrandMet's brewing group, with profits of £130 million, has only seven people in the divisional headquarters.

The money in these buildings is clearly not spent in the centre. The sparse boardroom at Clark's, for example, has a bare wooden table and unfilled cracks in the plaster. Yet almost next door lie the showrooms where buyers are introduced to new ranges of shoes – and here, where it matters, is where the money is spent. Daniel Clark's ancestors would have approved.

Hanson Trust's modest headquarters in Kensington also owes much to family tradition. Lord Hanson's father ran his substantial transport business without a headquarters building at all, which caused no end of headaches for the mandarins responsible for nationalizing the enterprise. 'Our people have a clear mandate with very little interference from headquarters,' he says.

The central London office block that houses Saatchi & Saatchi's headquarters staff is also home to a host of small operating units. Only about a dozen people carry out corporate functions, including Maurice Saatchi himself, and most of those are in finance.

The largest headquarters staff outside the retailing firms is Trusthouse Forte's 160. This includes a number of units such as pensions, property and hygiene, all of which are centralized. THF is an anomaly in this respect, occupying a midway position between the retailers and the fully decentralized manufacturers and service organizations.

All – including THF – spend considerable effort trying to keep down the size of HQ staff. Periodic examinations of who is at headquarters and why result in transfers back into the field. Above all, top management makes it clear that the route to promotion lies not in finding a comfortable niche in the centre, but in proving one's worth out in the field, where the money is made. Special privileges for headquarters staff are rare and indeed, loss of active bonuses may make transfer to headquarters unattractive in financial terms.

It is noticeable that successful turn-arounds frequently begin with the closure of lavish headquarters buildings in favour of smaller, less prestigious premises. This certainly was one of the first actions by Arnold Weinstock on taking over GEC (where numbers at company headquarters were cut from 2000 to 200 and now run at around 100), and has been an important plank of the turn-around programmes of Sir Michael Edwardes at BL and Ian MacGregor at British Steel. The motivation in all three cases was not simply the cash savings from selling off oversized offices, but the psychological impact of a restricted centre. Edwardes describes Leyland House, built to hold 1000 staff, as having 'no enthusiasm and a stifling atmosphere, rather like being in a luxury liner, without portholes; corridors between closed doors, behind which people seemed to work in a vacuum, at least two steps removed from the "nuts and bolts" of the business, which was in the Midlands, in Oxfordshire, in the north-west of England and in Scotland'.

Another sign of minimal bureaucracy is the relatively few levels between chairman and operating-unit head. Significantly, cutting these layers has been a main plank of many of the turn-arounds examined in Chapter 11.

Small, independent business units

'We are trying to create a small company environment in our units,' says Plessey's Parry Rogers. 'In a small unit, the people in charge know the employees, understand them and can be approached for explanations.'

Plessey's commitment to independent small units came from the realization in the early 1970s that the calibre of much of its management was inferior to its international competition. Explains Rogers: 'We set out ten years ago to change the quality of management in the company. The problem was measurable in two dimensions. The first was the competence and stature of the people we were able to attract into and develop towards top management. The second lay in the stability of the team. We had excessively high management turnover and a lot of people were reluctant to come to us. We had lesser men than we wanted in key positions.

'We concluded that the only way to attract the right people was to make management positions more attractive. At that time Plessey was very centralized, with a lot of decisions going to the top and a large corporate staff, which concerned itself (or interfered with) the decision-making process. The job of a manager in the middle of this pyramid was by no means as satisfying as that of the manager of a small company. The people the US competition placed in front of the customer were able to make decisions on their own authority. Ours couldn't.

'We felt we had to give people the authority to do their jobs. Our whole process of decentralization arose from this. Now we have boards of directors in all our subsidiaries, and make them responsible for the assets entrusted to them.' The middle managers capable of adaptation to an entrepreneurial environment, where they would have to show

33

leadership and take decisions on their own authority, thrived as they were moved out to head small profit centres. Those who could not adapt were gradually eased out. The headquarters staff is now down from hundreds to only forty.

At Racal, the decision to create small operating units arose because the company was beginning to lose the drive and enthusiasm that it had had as a collection of young men with a common ambition. Says a long-serving manager: 'In the early sixties Ray Brown and Ernest Harrison sat down and rethought their philosophy. The fifties had been a lot of fun, working till late and ending up in the pub before closing. But as the company grew, they realized they couldn't keep on doing this. How could they obtain the same sense of personal dedication and fun in a big company that they had when they were small?' The problem was brought into sharp focus by the relatively poor performance of two or three products as compared with the rest of the product portfolio, which then numbered about ten. Those that received less top-management attention tended to fare less well.

'The only way they could find to retain the original spirit was to re-create the original company as many times as possible,' says Kenneth Ward, 'and that was during a period when the prevailing trend was to make industrial companies bigger, to achieve economies of scale.

'By that time the headquarters site had grown to over a thousand people. From then on, with every new product we moved people elsewhere, starting up separate new units.' Racal has stuck rigidly to this approach ever since, splitting up units as they exceed the 500-employee mark, although in the case of its US acquisitions it has not been able to break up existing large manufacturing units in the short term.

'A small business has one product and a small team of people, who can be so intense in their interest that they get the best product and the best effort out of the people who work for them,' says Harrison. 'As you delegate you dilute that intensity.

'In a small unit you can keep that intensity alive. Everyone knows the costs, everyone knows the boss and everyone knows the customers. They see the boss all the time and he is one of them. They become family units, tight ships selling to the world.'

A small unit is also better equipped to deal with the small orders that add up to large profits. 'Central marketing gives priority to the big order of the day,' says Harrison. 'In a small company, they take the £10,000 order seriously.'

At Clark's the revelation came during World War Two, when the company had to give up its main factory for the production of torpedoes – hardly an event that went down well with its Quaker ethos. The mass-production halls were dispersed into numerous smaller buildings in the surrounding area. Productivity rose 250 per cent. Since then, Clark's has retained all its production in relatively small, semi-autonomous units.

Probably the best-known collection of small businesses in Britain is GEC, whose managing director Lord Weinstock has an almost pathological hatred of bureaucracy. The loose collection of a hundred and twenty or so companies that make up GEC have almost total autonomy as long as they meet their profit targets. The *Wall Street Journal* reported the new boss of GEC acquisition Picker International as having 'initial jitters that GEC would want to call the shots. Now he can laugh about it. Instead, he says, "It takes longer to get ideas through the Picker bureaucracy than it does through GEC."'

AGB has grown entirely out of small companies with high potential. 'We are more than eighty service companies in the group,' says chairman Bernard Audley. 'All the people in charge of these units have high autonomy. They'd leave if they didn't. Where we buy someone out, as we often do, we encourage them to stay and continue to grow the business by giving them cash now and more capital as the business grows.'

The arrangements with these managers are opportunistic and varied, but always contain a significant incentive for growth. 'Because of our policy of acquisition, I'd be suprised if less than 30 per cent of people in senior management positions had started up their own companies,' says Martin Ray, managing director of AGB subsidiary Langton Information Systems. 'I have three guys working for me who will be worth one and a half million pounds in a few years' time.'

At the Barratt group, new subsidiaries are split off amoeba-like as business in a profit centre reaches critical mass. Barratt fixes a maximum of 1000 houses built and sold in any one year within a single operating unit. When a profit centre expands to near the 1000 limit, it is split into two. Barratt aims in each case to achieve 25 per cent of the local house-building market, a feat he first accomplished in the north-east and is gradually repeating around the country.

'This business is all about local people and local management teams,' says Barratt. 'All our relationships with local communities are handled by the unit management.'

At Pritchard, the unit managers have 'no rigid styles and a great deal of freedom to take advantage of different business opportunities', says manager David Openshaw. Although each operating unit has a manual of how jobs are best done, top management's concern is focused not on how he does his job, but how well he performs against profit and growth targets. 'We aim at making subsidiaries substantial in their own right,' says Pritchard. 'And that needs an entrepreneurial type. Any fool can run a business, but it takes special people to build one.'

The retailers are in an unusual situation as the majority of their employees and assets are perforce distributed in a large number of small units. But the value of small, intimate teams is equally well recognized in the best performers. At Marks & Spencer, for example, Sieff and his colleagues agonized for years before finally giving the go-ahead for a third storey on the company's Marble Arch site, 'because it was too big. In the end, we decided to do it but to run the three floors as if each were a separate store.'

The situation in a conglomerate – or industrial management company as the multi-industry organizations in our sample prefer to be regarded – is different in that the independent units can actually be quite large. Even so, the tendency seems to be to break them down as much as possible, reflecting the freedoms given to the divisional company by the holding company board. BTR, for example, aims for a theoretical limit of 500 people on a site. Hanson Trust, for example, gives operating units almost complete control of their own affairs – as long, as we shall see in the next chapter, as they meet their financial targets and stick to a handful of corporate policies. 'We bend over backwards to avoid interfering in areas such as advertising or personnel,' says Peter Harper of its Allders subsidiary. Part of the process of absorbing a new company into the group is to push as much as possible of the centralized bureaucracy out into the field. At Allders, for example, treasury and property functions have now been moved into the stores. Hanson's brick operations also now push down as much as possible of the market intelligence-gathering to the local units, because they understand their own area.

The differences in the way these companies organize themselves to supervise the numerous small units are also interesting. Hanson Trust, for example, rigidly separates the holding company board from divisional management. 'It was laid down early on when we joined the group that we had no chance of joining the Hanson board while still in charge of a division,' says Dick Garrett.

The reason, explains Hanson, is to allow divisional managers to concentrate totally on the objectives of their units. At the same time, it frees the holding company board to allocate the investment cash at its disposal in a more dispassionate, objective way. 'In companies that put unit managers on the board, when one manager gets his cash he is well-disposed to let others with dog projects get theirs as well,' says Hanson. By contrast, adds Garrett, 'We are not bothered whether another division gets its capital budget; only whether we get ours.' If nothing else, this strict separation of responsibilities reduces the opportunity for corporate politicking.

The Barratt group adopts a more traditional style of organization, with each of its regions controlled by a main board director, who acts as chairman of a five-man board. The main board comprises Sir Lawrie himself, the five regional directors, the finance director and the sales/marketing director. The seven to ten subsidiaries in each region are represented on the regional boards.

Informal systems of working together

Large numbers of independent units can all too easily create confusion, perhaps bidding against each other for the same contract, or poaching key managers away from each other. The problem for the chief executive of the decentralized company is to impose sufficient regulation on the enterprises to prevent too much damage being done, yet without hampering the entrepreneurial spirit of the units by, say, obliging them to buy at above-market prices from other group members.

Clark's, for example, will not require its retail outlets to buy from other factories within the group if they can buy cheaper and better elsewhere. 'It all stems from the freedom for each company to do what it feels is right,' says Malcolm Cotton, managing director of Clark's Ltd. The company even goes so far as to keep the pressure on manufacturing units by deliberately buying from outside suppliers: although it developed polyurethane and has the capacity to supply all its needs if it wanted to, it buys in 25 per cent of its supplies from external manufacturers.

In the rare instances where disputes arise between units as a result of this independent behaviour, the chairman arbitrates. 'My office then has to try to balance autonomy against inter-trade between the units,' says Daniel Clark.

At Plessey, Sir John Clark establishes with each business unit its product charter – a smaller, more detailed version of the corporate mission. Within the charter they can act with considerable freedom. 'But if they want to go outside it, either with a new product or an acquisition, they have to come up with a strategic investment plan,' he explains. This formal notification allows top management to identify and assess any potential conflicts arising from two units competing for the same market.

GEC accepts that a certain amount of competitive bidding will take place by its subsidiaries, although Weinstock insists that a US report that five GEC subsidiaries had bid for the same contract is untrue. 'We encourage units to work together where appropriate,' he says. 'But if two units bid for the same contracts frequently and one always wins out, then there's a lesson to be learned.'

Action-oriented, informal management teams

'We don't work on a committee basis at all. We have virtually no formal meetings. We deal with things as they arise, in small teams. Some people find it hard to believe we can make a major move here when the chairman is in California, but decisions have to be made wherever the key directors are,' says Hanson Trust director John Pattisson.

In the early days at Bejam all the directors worked together in one office, with a desk in each corner so they could each see what the others were doing. If a problem or opportunity arose, they were able to form a huddle and decide quickly what to do. Even though they now have individual offices, they are close together so that the swift team decision can still be made.

Somewhere in the building, says finance director John Edwards, there is an envelope covered with calculations, on which the directors worked out the costs of running the company's own freezer insurance scheme, then a major innovation. It took a matter of hours from the first suggestion to sealing the decision and not much longer to implement it.

'All our acquisitions have been very fast,' says GrandMet's Grinstead. 'In the case of Express Dairy, for example, the approach was made at four p.m.; by four p.m. the next day we had committed ourselves.' It was, he admits, a considerable risk, because although the deal gave GrandMet control of the company, it only held a very small proportion of the shares.

Much the same happened in the £500 million acquisition of Intercontinental Hotels in 1981. Recalls Grinstead: 'I went over to see Pan Am and asked if they would sell us the hotel chain. They said, "No!" Then a few weeks later they came to us and said, "Would you like to talk?" I discussed it with all the members of the board and they basically felt comfortable about it. Max Joseph was ill in the South of France. I had lunch with him and he felt OK about it too. In New York we spent from Sunday to Thursday hammering it out. I spoke to everyone on the Grand-Met board about the price before we concluded the deal.' It took less than a week from opportunity to signature.

MFI has a reputation for being particularly swift on its feet when it comes to obtaining and developing sites for new stores. 'We are very action-oriented,' says an MFI manager. 'We call it "sense of urgency". We can move from signing the contract on a piece of land to opening the store in six months. A building programme for a 40,000-square-foot store would normally take forty-four weeks; it takes us twenty-six.'

'Management by huddle', as it might be called, seems to run across the top strata of our successful companies. There is an avoidance of committees, except as a means of consultation, to bring everyone in on a decision they will have to work with. ('I don't like committees; I don't work with them,' says GrandMet's Grinstead.) Instead, at the very top, our successful companies rely on a depth of mutual understanding and agreement on where the company is going and what is right. There is often no need to engage in length discussion – everyone knows whether something fits the culture and the objectives of the organization. It is, perhaps, a sign of the clear management mission we touched upon in the previous chapter.

This kind of intuitive teamwork comes out in STC, for example, in the regular annual presentation to line managers. Explains Alex Park: 'The most important thing we have is a form of communication that gives us a management bond. I've worked in seven companies, on both sides of the Atlantic, and I've never seen anything like it.

'For our management information meetings, each member of the executive team is given the general topic in a heading of four or five words, plus a few words relating to his area of responsibility, of about the same length. We never converse with each other about our slides or our script. It amazes me, but it always hangs together. The seven or eight speakers have common themes and a clear understanding of their roles.' Despite the lack of discussion on content, there are almost never clashes or duplications. 'Because it happens at the top level, it cascades down,' says Park. 'Much the same happens in other meetings we hold.'

Part of the secret here is that everyone at top-management level spends a lot of time just bouncing ideas off his colleagues, even though they may come from completely different disciplines. Another part is that no one is proprietary about his area of responsibility. 'In STC everyone interferes with everyone in what everyone else does and no one resents it. They are prepared to listen to anyone,' says Duncan Lewis of Corfield's office. Other success stories outside our sample also show similar behaviour at the top. One of the ingredients in the gradual turn-around of one of Britain's most run-down retail chains, Woolworth, is that the new team operates with an absence of formality or territorial protection. 'It's expected that we become involved in each others' areas,' says company secretary Nigel Whittaker. 'But ultimately, the decision is theirs, and once it is made, we will back them, whatever has been said before.'

Both Lord Forte and Rocco Forte have tried to develop a similar team, and to push it down the line. Rocco frequently calls line managers several levels below to find out the background to a problem or opportunity. 'I don't issue instructions down the line, but I get information better at source,' he explains.

Lord Weinstock is famous for doing the same. 'I want to know what's happening,' he explains. 'If I can identify someone specific to speak to, I'll telephone him. I won't go to his boss if I want to find out, for example, why the man didn't answer a letter.' The members of the GEC top executive team also make a practice of circulating the letters and telexes they receive, to keep each other informed.

This informality and lack of bureaucracy in day to day operations can be seen in the way executives in these companies get things done. Very few of them give orders. Indeed, Daniel Clark's co-directors had to think hard before they could remember an occasion when he had ever done so. 'I'd only issue an order as a last resort. If you issue orders, you take away people's ability to think for themselves,' says STC's Corfield.

'The STC management board almost never makes decisions,' says Lewis. 'Decisions are taken all over the place by groups given the responsibility. It means spending an immense amount of time giving people a wide understanding of company objectives. But with a lot of people doing groundwork, thinking about it, the formal decision can be implemented very fast.'

Rather than issue instructions, says Plessey's Sir John Clark, 'I do a personal critique of every profit and loss account each quarter. I sit with people to evolve policies and strategies for their unit.' When he does give orders, it is because someone has jeopardized the effectiveness of his operation by consistently ignoring advice. 'For example, I had to tell one of our top designers to go to Egypt to see how his product was being used.'

Lord Weinstock is pulled up sharp by a co-director when he says he, too, rarely gives orders. He does admit to making very strong suggestions. 'I've had rows with people where I've said, "Don't do it – but it's your responsibility, your decision." I don't remember which way they decided in the end.'

Delegation all down the line

'Centralization implies that people cannot be trusted,' says Hanson Trust's Garrett. If that is so, the autonomy philosophy implies that people should be trusted by delegating responsibility to the lowest level where people can use it effectively. According to David Clarke, president of Hanson Industries in the United States: '99 per cent of all decisions are taken locally.'

The young Charles Forte learnt the lesson early. 'When I expanded to a second milk bar I had to leave a woman in charge of the first. She ran it better than I did. If I hadn't given her her head, I wouldn't have 40,000 employees now. I'd still have twelve.'

Clark's of Street delegates almost all day-to-day and short-term decisions, according to a management consultant who knows the company well. Long-term decisions, however, are normally taken in the centre. 'Strategy is very centralized, tactics very decentralized,' he explains. 'At one time there were thirty plants in the west of England. All could buy equipment, change factory layout and so on as long as it fitted a centrally decided policy of what should be made where.'

Says United Biscuits' Robert Clark: 'While major variations from the total business plan will need to be discussed, people are given a very free hand. There's no one breathing down their necks.'

'What this means in practice is that the site manager has very great autonomy. It's just not possible in our business to lay down a production plan for a year. We do have general guidelines, however. This year a key objective is not to put up unit labour costs, for example.'

While concerned to retain central control over most aspects of store operation, Asda's chief executive John Hardman is strenuously trying to introduce more of this kind of attitude. Until recently a somewhat autocratic organization, Asda now has to bring its managers to the stage where instead of being told what to do they can work out what to do themselves. The inability of managers to accept delegation was threatening to halt the pace of the company's growth at the end of the 1970s. The scale of the problem is perhaps illustrated by the tale of the hapless assistant store manager who was telephoned by the company mimic, pretending to be one of the company controllers. 'Move the food department to the non-food area and vice versa by eight o'clock tonight,' the mimic ordered. It was carried out without question.

A positive attitude towards risk-taking

Persuading managers to take initiatives is one of the more difficult tasks for any top-management team. Doing so involves both providing incentives to take controlled, calculated risks and removing the fear of failure.

This is against a background where experience has taught managers in many British companies that risk-taking does not pay off and that career success comes more surely from restraining those imaginative leaps ahead than from embracing them with enthusiasm.

Among the ways in which companies discourage initiatives and risk-taking are the following:

- they insist on reviewing all risk decisions at a high level. As a result, line managers pass up the buck, knowing that someone above will take the responsibility
- they impose financial controls with too little leeway. Managers find that they do not have the discretionary spending power to take initiatives of their own accord
- they have excessively rigid rules and procedures. Risk ventures often, by their nature, involve a departure from the rules
- by expecting a guaranteed return. Risk ventures, again by their nature,

will not always come off. But many companies kill off new ventures before they start by insisting that they contain no risks

- they penalize managers when the risk does not come off. The manager whose risk venture fails may expect delayed promotion, or to be shunted aside, or even to be fired in many companies
- they do not provide enough rewards for success. Sometimes the down-side risk to the manager is outweighed by the possible increase in stature or remuneration if he succeeds – but not often. 'In the West at least,' says Tom Lossius of the Conference Board in Brussels, 'risk-taking is not worth the candle. The risks are great but the rewards are not commensurate.' A survey by *International Management* magazine, published in December 1983, showed that nearly two-fifths of British managers were inhibited from taking risks by insufficient rewards. Just under 28 per cent were put off by the penalties for failure
- by the example set by top management. If the executive directors do not take the company into calculated risks, then people down the line are unlikely to stick out their necks. If they talk about success as simply hitting the budget, they will never encourage people to reach out beyond the budget to seize new and unexpected opportunities.

Our successful companies generally present a picture that is the antithesis of all this. They typically allow the line manager to take whatever risks he deems necessary, within his budget and limits of authority.

The successful companies do maintain strict control of finance, as we shall see in the next chapter. But they encourage managers to make out the case for unbudgeted expenditures and, if the project receives the go-ahead, back them to the hilt. They also permit a certain amount of breaking the rules, where it can later be justified. The key, says United Biscuits executive Robert Clark, is that top management must be informed of what is being done and why, so that if things do go wrong, it does not come as an unpleasant surprise. 'The only sin you can commit in United Biscuits is not to let the top know when there is bad news,' he declares.

These companies also recognize that some risks have to fail, but are prepared to look at them as learning experiences. Pritchard managers often deliberately allow a subordinate to try things his own way, even though they know it carries an abnormally high risk of failure, simply to give the employee the chance to learn for himself. 'We give people a lot of support if they make mistakes,' says a Pritchard manager. Where a new venture goes wrong, they expect the manager concerned to accept full responsibility. But the only penalty to the manager is that it probably affects the profitability of his unit and therefore the size of his bonus. On the other side of the coin, if the venture is a success and contributes to increased profitability, this is normally reflected in his pay packet, too.

This attitude encourages people to admit their mistakes, rather than hide them until they become too big to conceal. 'I've known very senior people come in and say, "I've cocked this up. Do you want my resignation?"' says GrandMet's Grinstead. The offer has never been taken up.

'Sir Hector will always back people when they make mistakes, providing they have honestly tried,' says United Biscuits' Robert Clark. 'In the only other company I've worked for people would be sacked for things that here would earn them a pat on the back and "Well, you tried". The managers who were in our failed cake business have all advanced. Sir Hector is not looking for sacrificial heads when things go wrong – but only a man who is really in control of his company can play it that way.'

Daniel Clark recalls how one manager worked out the idea for a different kind of shop. 'It was a big unit, where a large space off centre was set aside for discount sales. We tried it with two experimental shops. It didn't work, although we did it right.'

'I was still pleased he tried it. I'd have been a lot more worried if he had been afraid to launch into it.'

The problems arise when managers fail frequently or when they are asked to take over a troubled area of the company, where there is a high risk of finding themselves presiding over a business calamity. In the first case, claim many of our successful companies, a manager has to demonstrate a consistent pattern of failure in new ventures, before he will be removed. Even then, the chances are high that he will be moved into a position where entrepreneurial flair is not required. In the second case, our sample companies tend to raise the rewards for success in turnarounds so that they more than match the personal risks.

Above all, these companies show they mean business by the scale of the risks they themselves initiate. It takes considerable courage, for example, to put the business on the line for a single major project in the Middle East, as Pritchard did in 1976. But the cleaning company's preplanning of the requirements for street cleaning in Riyadh was so thorough that the real risks were reduced. In order to assess the real volumes of rubbish that would have to be collected from homes and institutions in a city where no cleaning service existed, where there were no street maps and where most houses had no numbers, Pritchard sent a team of employees to walk the streets estimating the dustcart requirements of each home.

The attitude of being willing to take risks penetrates down the line to the unit managers, who bring in new growth opportunities. Many of these opportunities are acquisitions of smaller companies. 'We take very quick decisions on these acquisitions,' says Peter Pritchard. 'We encourage the local managers to seek out suitable organizations. It gives an extra dimension to their jobs.' Alert local managers were involved in over a hundred such acquisitions one recent year.

Saatchi & Saatchi goes to great lengths to minimize cash risks. 'We don't really take *any* financial risks; we are almost too cautious financially,' says Maurice Saatchi. At the same time, it recognizes that growth and innovation depend on a lot of people independently taking small calculated risks. It creates the environment where this can happen by splitting the company into two. On the one side are the multiple small operating units responsible for the creative work, for dreaming up big ideas. On the other is the finance department, which is clearly separated but has to be consulted before ideas that mean spending cash can be put into practice. These two mutually opposing forces produce a working compromise, in which each has to understand the thinking of the other. 'The pull between them is very healthy,' says Saatchi.

Generalist managers

Several (but not all) of our successful companies also extol the virtues of generalist managers. Functional specialization may be useful, but a good manager should be able to transcend his early training and obtain a much broader grasp of management, they believe. 'I don't believe the profession of a leader matters one iota,' says Harrison. 'He just has to surround himself with the right team. Ray Brown was an engineer; I am an accountant by training. When I took over as group managing director, I made sure that the unit managing directors were engineers.' In this way, any lack of detailed technical knowledge on his part becomes irrelevant, he believes, because the technical resource is still strong within the top-management team.

The companies who responded to our written questionnaire appeared, by and large, to have given very little thought to the issue of generalist versus specialist managers. None considered themselves outstanding in this respect and only two (Smiths Industries and Wm Morrison Supermarkets) thought they were above average. Although there are examples of companies which have suffered severe problems because the top management is heavily engineering-based and unable to cope with marketing issues, there are equally examples of companies which have failed to manage innovation because they did not have the technical expertise and understanding at the top. The same applies to other disciplines, such as finance.

One possible conclusion from this might be that safety lies in achieving as broad as possible a background at senior management and board level.

Summary

Even where they are heavily centralized, our successful companies convince line managers that they do in fact have considerable autonomy. In any company, a manager's freedom to act is set against a background of restraints, some of them imposed from the outside, such as market conditions, technological limitations or the cost of money, others imposed from within the organization. Somehow, these companies create an atmosphere where constraints are often turned on their head and seen instead as opportunities. This applies particularly to the control mechanisms exercised down the line by top management. There may be a great many strings attached to the individual manager, but he often has considerable reach before they are pulled upon.

United Biscuits' Robert Clark expresses it in this way: 'Autonomy is often there more in the feeling than in the reality. We have a lot of controls, but still they feel they are almost completely independent. Somehow we engender the feeling in them that they are running their own businesses.'

How this works – the exercise of tight controls within a framework where initiative and autonomy are encouraged in some aspects of the job and discouraged in others – we shall discuss next.

4 Control

'Successful companies take charge of their own destiny' –
Daniel Clark

One immediate observation of most of our successful companies, which contrasts with many unsuccessful companies, is that they try hard to keep central controls to a minimum compatible with the fulfilment of their objectives. To be able to do that, of course, they must first have a very clear understanding of what those objectives are. Because people further down also understand the broad objectives, it is rare for these companies to use their control systems for slamming on the brakes. On the contrary, the successful company is rather like a lively horse and trap where both the animal and the driver know where they are going. All that is needed is an occasional gentle tug at the reins.

That doesn't mean that the controls are lax. Quite the opposite in fact. As a general rule, it seems that the fewer controls exercised by the centre, the more strictly line managers are expected to adhere to them.

What they choose to control depends to a large extent on the industry, the company structure and the company culture. With few exceptions, all have very tight controls on capital expenditure. In addition STC and Racal, for example, have strong controls on technology – an obvious measure in an industry where staying ahead in technological terms is essential to survival. Sainsbury is almost pathological about hygiene, organizing regular inspections in which each store is scored and any manager who fails an inspection is harried until he raises his standards to the required level.

It is also noticeable that these companies often use the carrot as well as the stick to ensure that these crucial controls are observed. The relationship between cash controls and personal rewards is often close, for example, and the culture of the company often tends to ensure that the manager who responds most effectively to the controls – indeed, who uses them as aids in the fulfilment of his unit's objectives – will be recognized and drawn up the promotional ladder.

Indeed, as we hinted at the end of the previous chapter, what counts is often the perception of the manager himself. Does he see the control system as a constricting pincer that prevents him from moving in the directions he knows to be best for his unit? Or does he see it as a necessary constraint that frees him to concentrate his efforts on the things that really matter?

Plessey, for example, treats its control systems as a means of rationalizing delegation of authority. Explains finance director Peter Marshall: 'We have found a way of distinguishing between decisions that have to be made at the centre and those that must be made in the operating units, in such a way that the two are never in conflict.

'If you take a conventional balance sheet, you list freehold assets, plant, stock, debtors, cash and so on. We have decided that some of these areas are corporate issues which should be dealt with centrally and others should be left to the man on the spot. All our unit managing directors are dealing with trade. Their success criterion is profitability derived from trade, pre-tax and irrespective of source of funds. For a contract he writes that meets corporate criteria he will, for example, be able to carry a certain level of stock. All he has to do is deliver on time, to the customer's satisfaction.

'If he wants to do anything exceptional, he has to seek corporate permission. If he wants to extend customer credit, for example, he has to go to our own finance company, which provides the credit for his business. It works like a charm because it takes a lot of the weight off his shoulders.

'The aim of the centre is to help the unit manager get on with his job. Our managing directors don't know the first thing about tax; nor about currency. They deal only in the currency of the country where they are. The system is designed to leave the maximum time for matters concerned with selling and producing. It helps them to become specialists in their marketplace rather than generalists in things such as company law.'

The controls are usually very simple and the reasons for having them very obvious in most of our successful companies. Top management concentrates on a small number of key ratios or results that are particularly significant to their business and reacts to anomalies immediately and directly. Even Lord Weinstock, famed for his control methods, receives all the basic information he needs on three sheets of paper, from which he can tell at a glance if something is seriously amiss. He compares it with a radiologist reading an X-ray: after years of experience the anomalies stand out straight away.

The speed with which they insist on receiving certain financial information (with next-working-day reporting now becoming increasingly common) goes a long way to convincing managers down the line that the controls are an important part of the company culture. Controls become less obtrusive – indeed, often unobtrusive – if they are simple enough to become automatic and if the culture makes them highly relevant to the manger's own immediate job. If the information is needed internally anyway, it becomes almost a matter of obligatory courtesy to send it on to headquarters, too.

The simplicity and astuteness of the control system is frequently seen as the key to some of our successful businesses. GEC, for example, controls cash and bureaucracy. Units are given very wide autonomy while they perform, and performance is monitored through comprehensive reporting systems. Any unit that fails to perform sees its autonomy swiftly vanish.

This is how Paul Johnson, writing in *The Director* magazine (December 1983), saw the Weinstock system of controls:

A federated business, which allows managers great independence in decision-making, will only work if central finance supervision is fierce, continuous and intelligent. Weinstock's method is not unlike the system of Treasury Control, which managed British government so successfully until social aims took priority over financial probity.

Every GEC company has its own bank account. It cannot draw on central funds and must provide its own finance for normal capital spending. Every month it must make a cash contribution to central funds in accordance with its budget forecasts. Above all, it must supply head office with a continuous flow of precise financial information. It is not just that, every single day, HQ examines cash balances or overdrafts of all companies. It is that Weinstock believes figures cannot lie if presented in accordance with precise and meaningful instructions. Managers must include the following basic ratios in their progress-summaries: sales to capital, profits to sales, profits to capital, sales to stocks, sales to debtors and sales per employee. Weinstock studies these figures avidly and often writes down the key digits on bits of paper. Any company whose figures do not satisfy him will soon get a phone call and must give a convincing account of what steps it has taken to put things right. Weinstock can be very blunt, and the annual budget sessions in which he and his senior colleagues cross-examine managers are exacting affairs. In the last resort, Weinstock believes, the only real controls are financial ones and to be effective they must be speedy and continuous. He thus provides an early warning system for the entire business, which ensures that action is taken the moment errors are revealed by the financial monitor.

However, Weinstock maintains, perhaps a little tongue-in-cheek, that 'we should be known for our lack of controls. This company is an amalgamation of several companies, all of which – except for the one I came from – were in serious trouble. Without serious [financial] disciplines they would all have gone to the wall. We started to impose disciplines and we became famous for the systems we evolved to make sure we did survive. We still use the same mechanical forms of reporting, of daily returns of cash. But now they are used to promote dialogue with people in the business.'

Lord Forte, too, sees financial controls as the key to his company's growth. Says a company biography:

> He had worked out his own business philosophy and applied it meticulously to his first venture. This was based on a strict analysis of the potential of the business – of turnover, gross profit, wages and other expenses and the resultant net profit – having decided what the minimum must be to make it a viable proposition. He applied his yardstick to compare one operation with another by the use of percentages or ratios. He describes it as a simple system yet believes that without it he might still be controlling a very limited operation.

Certain themes tend to arise again and again in discussing control systems with the top management of these companies. These are:

- tight controls on finance, to ensure that the money goes where it will be most effective in generating more
- constant feedback of results
- close attention to business planning
- setting high standards and expecting people to stick to them

Tight controls on finance

At Hanson Trust the standing joke is that any manager who asks to buy a new typewriter will receive a note from the group chairman telling him to check first whether there is a spare machine at Whetstone, where Berec used to occupy the whole of a large headquarters building. The capital amount may seem absurdly trivial to occupy the attention of the chairman of a £1.5 billion company. But every request for unbudgeted capital expenditure in excess of £500 is automatically routed through group headquarters, and, as with company cars and salaries above £20,000, has to be approved by Lord Hanson.

The Hanson philosophy stresses that unit managers should have almost total freedom to run their units as they like – except where cash is concerned. Rigid reporting procedures allow top management to detect quickly whether any business is going off course, and to take corrective action.

For Ever Ready, for example, regular reporting means sales results down to gross margin every week and budgets broken down for comparison with the same week in the previous year. The salesmen also get a regional profit and loss account every month. Ever Ready Ltd's managing director Michael Johnson finds that the scrutiny exercised by the centre on these figures always tends to be pessimistic rather than optimistic about apparently positive trends, in order to keep the unit managers' feet on the ground. This leads to a good deal of humorous repartee between the group accountants and the operating units. On one occasion when the South African subsidiary had a particularly good pre-Christmas week, it received a telex telling it not to be too pleased with itself, because snow had depressed sales the corresponding week of the previous year!

Like Hanson Trust, Trafalgar House insists that newly acquired companies adopt its strict financial controls from day one of new ownership. Detailed reports from each unit, covering the current state and projections for cash, capital expenditure, employees, sales turnover and profits, are condensed into a 100-page monthly summary for the executive committee. Cash-flow forecasts for five years ahead allow chairman Sir Nigel Broackes and managing director Eric Parker to plan the growth of the company by internal development and timed acquisitions. To stress that the budgets really are meant as a planning tool, Trafalgar House jargon refers to them as blueprints.

Financial controls were essential in turning round companies such as Cunard (which was effectively bankrupt at the time of its takeover) and Dorman Long (which was heavily loss-making under British Steel and is now one of the first successful transfers from state to private sector ownership). Strict controls have also been applied to Scott Lithgow, which cost the taxpayer over £200 million since nationalization, but which Trafalgar House predicts will become profitable.

One of the main reasons for such close watching of the figures is to prevent subsidiaries cutting margins too much in order to buy business – a frequent cause of company collapse in the engineering and construction industries that form the bulk of the group.

Plessey's sharp division of responsibilities between the centre and the operating units is accompanied by a financial control procedure based on return on assets managed (ROAM). Simply put, every unit is charged a monthly sum based on the expected ROAM. The managing director is expected to run the operation so that it still makes a profit after that deduction. This sharpens his attention on the assets under his control, and discourages him from accumulating additional assets that may not pay back at the level demanded. It also means that a positive profit and loss account is more likely to be in the form of cash than stock. The system is described by external observers as 'rigid and rigorous'.

However generous it may be in its incentive payments, MFI exercises tight control over expenses. Employees are not even permitted to charge a daily newspaper to their hotel bill – and check-out receipts are scrutinized to make sure they do not. AGB, too, tempers the exceptional freedom it allows unit managing directors to run their companies as they like by holding tight to the purse strings on expensive items such as long-distance travel. 'Our kind of entrepreneurial manager would get on a plane at the drop of a hat, if it meant getting to grips with a problem,' says Audley. 'We try to strike the best balance that we can between freedom and controls.' A group manual covers this and other criteria such as levels of secretarial and clerical staff, which can easily get out of hand under an entrepreneurial manager.

The company that keeps the loosest rein on capital expenditure is Bulmer, where, says Nelson, 'Once they have a budget, managers have almost total discretion on how they spend it.' Nelson can authorize capital expenditure of up to £250,000 without reference to the board; his immediate subordinates can authorize up to £150,000. Once given a budget, the manager has the freedom to spend it as he likes within the constraints of his agreed objectives. None the less, he has to ensure that the centre knows what he is doing and it is debatable whether this kind of approach would work as well in an organization with a variety of products and plants in different geographical areas.

Constant feedback of results

At Pritchard each operating unit is budgeted against a report thirteen times a year. 'A person knows whether he's a success or not by the facts, on a regular basis,' says a middle manager. 'We discuss the figures openly. It's almost like a league table.'

Barratt feeds back top management's view of each month's figures in marathon twelve- to fourteen-hour management meetings, chaired by a main-board director. The agenda for the meeting is the monthly report from the operating unit, which is submitted to the regional headquarters in a standard form. Group headquarters also receives the same information. Each unit obtains its funding from a group banking, which assigns them overdraft facilities just as a normal bank would do.

Racal makes sure that 'even the most junior managers are aware of the financial situation' after the four-weekly profit and loss accounts. None the less, says Harrison, 'a good manager knows how he has done at the end of the week without a P&L. Historic accounting just confirms what you should already know.'

Close attention to business planning

Sir John Clark sees Plessey's planning system as crucial to his company's survival and growth during the past decade. Planning at Plessey is a constantly evolving process, always aiming to come closer to the real course of future events and to influence developments rather than be forced to react to them. Sir John explains how planning developed in Plessey as follows: 'We started with *financial* planning systems – which weren't really planning at all. Then we got into Boston Consulting analysis. I am a great believer in the experience curve. Then we introduced an objective- and strategy-setting system from Texas Instruments, followed by a General Electric system of competitive analysis, where you decide which are your strategic business units. In this system, you compare for management and economic power with your competitors. You have to be at least fourth in the competitive race to get anywhere. The theory can be overdone, but it's a good starting point.

'We use competitive analysis to ensure that the learning curve is not undermined by someone else coming in with brand-new technology. Now we are going over the organization of our planning yet again. I want to take organizational matters away from personnel. We are developing software systems that will intelligently identify strategic business units, and throw up criticisms of their policy and position, together with suggestions of what we should do to make them more competitive.'

One other aspect of Plessey's approach to strategic planning is worthy of note. The financial aspect of planning has been progressively downgraded in relation to the commercial and technological aspects. The planning structure begins with the marketplace and the changes necessary to compete there. Only when the commercial plan is conceived in outline are the financial forecasts added, to determine whether it will be economically feasible. The final objectives are always expressed in commercial rather than financial terms. The importance of the technology aspect of planning is reflected in the combination of planning and technology under one director – with a technological background.

AGB's Audley, on the other hand, says: 'I've tried corporate planning (the formal kind) with only moderate success. The opportunities for a company like ours to plan ahead in detail are much smaller than for a company with a heavy industrial base. Instead, our planning comes from continuing discussion about each business with close colleagues. We are aware of the scene around us; we create a general matrix, often a worldwide matrix. Then we achieve a consensus on which way to go.'

These two companies typify the extremes of approach to strategic planning. One relies on the detailed but relatively flexible five-year plan to set visible targets and define routes to achieve them. It achieves its goals by following the plan as far as possible and revising its route (and sometimes the objectives too) at least every year, and usually on a continuous basis. Growth is primarily organic and internal, rather than by acquisition.

The other can best be described as an opportunistic approach, which sets broad-brush objectives, commits everyone to achieving them, and seizes any chance to move towards them. This approach relies heavily on the availability of cash resources, generated from operations that are already successful. Unit managers are constantly evaluating new projects, from which further growth may come, instead of concerning themselves deeply about the operational problems of their unit as it is. Their growth focus tends to be more external, through buying in talented people who have new ideas and financing their efforts, or through direct acquisition of smaller companies with the potential to expand.

Both these strategies are offensive rather than defensive. Our success-ful companies spend noticeably less time complaining about unfair competition from Japan, the United States or the Third World than do the less successful end of their industry sectors.

Strategic planning at STC starts with a top-level committee on which sit both directors and the corporate planners. 'We take planning and action to shape the future very seriously. We try to be as realistic about the future as is possible,' says Cooper. 'At one time our planning would all be done by economists. Then line managers would ignore it, or dis-agree with their conclusions. So we combined top management and planning specialists in one committee. We have heated debates on some issues, but we come out of them with a decision that represents the experience of the managers and the expert knowledge of the specialists.

'This approach means we get a lot nearer to what actually happens than we used to. In addition, we all feel involved and committed to it. If it goes wrong we can all make corrections together.'

Corfield defines business planning as 'the most efficient achievement of the possible'. The STC plan starts with the identification of the re-sources available internally, externally and jointly with another com-pany, and what could be done with them. Then comes the process of testing for credibility, in which the broad objectives are turned into a detailed two-year and less detailed five-year plan. Each unit's plan has its assumptions tested by a wide variety of functional experts, as well as by more senior managers. The idea is to prevent individual vested inter-ests from clouding the issue and to ensure that problems are not hidden.

Unit managers prepare their objectives for the next year between January and April. Between April and September the plans are con-solidated, tested and re-tested until they are ready for review by every-one concerned with them, *en masse*. These review meetings often include up to a hundred people. From this review of the plan next year's budget is derived, for approval in December.

The constant cycle – a legacy of ITT – means that planning is far from a once-a-year binge that gets buried immediately afterwards as managers get back to the practical realities of running a business. The constant evaluation and re-evaluation of the planning assumptions is reinforced by monthly forecasts by each unit manager, which update expectations with the benefit of a much closer perspective. By comparing these 'real-time' expectations with the budget, major and minor deviant trends can be detected swiftly. Action taken depends on how serious the deviation is. If it is relatively minor, it is simply monitored in much closer detail to ensure that it does not get out of hand. If it is major, it sparks off a reworking of the plan, using much the same procedures as for the original, only condensed into a much shorter time period.

GrandMet uses strategic planning as the basic starting point for turning around any loss-making company it acquires. Its acquisition of a tobacco company in the United States brought it a motley collection of businesses, most of which had been poorly managed. In the event, however, it was the tobacco company which was disposed of and the best of the other companies that were retained. 'The American owners managed their portfolio like a game of poker, drawing and discarding,' says Grinstead. 'All of those companies are now operating better than before. Within three months of the acquisition I'd visited all of them. We made them think about strategy, about opportunities and risks for their businesses. Then they have to give us a thirty-six-hour presentation about their company. At the end of the exercise I feel comfortable (or not) about the management and what they are doing.'

Saatchi & Saatchi is one of the few companies to quote other company chairmen in its annual report. This is what it highlighted from a speech by Sir Hector Laing: 'In reaching our present position we have succeeded in achieving the essential goals we set in our strategic plan. Where we have adhered to our strategic principles whether applied to acquisition or to quality of product or management, we have been successful.

'We have failed when we have ignored or compromised those principles. That is the most important lesson of these years.'

Setting high standards and expecting people to stick to them

At GEC, managers who do not make sufficiently ambitious plans can expect to feel the full opprobrium of failure. The company mythology includes the tale of a hapless executive, who was put in charge of a loss-making unit. He put together a turn-around plan, which made it clear that a good return on assets could not be expected for some time. At budget time, the new managing director and his finance director were summoned for the traditional annual review meeting with Lord Weinstock.

The two men sat expectantly on the other side of the desk as Weinstock leafed through the pages of their plan. The chairman's lips curled progressively downwards as he read on. Suddenly, he put his head in his hands on the desk and said, 'You guys make me feel sick.' Silence followed as the two executives waited for Weinstock to continue. After several minutes, the two rose quietly and tiptoed shamefacedly out of the room, leaving him still silent and head bowed. Although the tale is probably heavily embroidered, it encapsulates the demand for managers to extend themselves towards challenging objectives.

None of our other successful company chairmen adopt quite such dramatic ways of getting the point across. But all are very demanding in the standards of performance they expect from their managers. Racal, for example, presses its unit managers for 25 per cent growth in sales and return on assets each year. Trafalgar House, too, is very demanding. 'High standards are set in every conceivable way,' claims W.B. Slater, chairman of Trafalgar subsidiary Cunard Shipping Services. 'We don't tolerate second-rate performance,' Lord Hanson adds to the chorus.

Clark's Quaker philosophy has never prevented it from setting very tough profit goals. 'They put profit first and look after people as a result of making profits,' says Cotton. The shoe company also sees high profit levels as essential for the maintenance of investment, in the absence of recourse to the capital markets. 'We talk all the time of profits versus assets employed.'

'High standards', says a PA consultant familiar with the company, 'are the essence of Clark's controls.'

STC's Corfield preaches a system of decision-making that always pushes managers just that little bit harder than they might have pushed themselves. 'The way to make decisions', he explains, 'is to decide what the perfect solution is, then what the possible solution is, then compromise between them.'

Perhaps the most effective way that top management puts across the high standards it requires is by its own example. 'If anyone arrives here at seven-twenty in the morning and bumps into Sir Hector,' says United Biscuits' Robert Clark, 'he would assume they were late. Why not, when he himself is always here early in the morning?' Not surprisingly, other managers follow suit.

Saatchi's annual reports consistently stress a number of values that imply constant reaching for higher standards. 'One of our 30-second commercials for a product should be worth 60 seconds of advertising from its competitor', it boasts, adding that it has '*a belief in excellence* – that in all spheres of life and at all times there will be a few performances which are excellent, a few which are very poor ... while the majority will be just average.

'Our aim in all of our activities and at all times is *the avoidance of the average and the achievement of the excellent*. This applies to all aspects of the way we run our business – to the people we employ, to the advertising we run, to the way we buy our media, to the operating margins we expect.

'All our standards are set by the "norm" – whatever that is, by definition, there is a better way.'

Most of the high standards in our successful companies evolve after careful thought and assessment against fundamental business objectives. Some, however, originate in single, dramatic gestures. Staff at Asda tell the apocryphal tale of the manager of a new superstore, waiting outside the premises for the executives to arrive for the official opening. As the light plane bringing the executives to the ceremony flew overhead, the manager was amazed to hear a voice booming from above telling him to clear up the mess in the store's backyard. The point, that the public image demanded cleanliness and tidiness outside the store as well as inside, was not lost on him nor on other branch managers.

Summary

The tension between control and independence is inevitable. What our most successful companies seem to have done is use that tension constructively to create a feeling of maximum autonomy while keeping tight rein on the areas that matter for their market and type of organization. All freedom is relative; it brings with it responsibilities, which of themselves become restraints. Creating the right framework of control and independence is one of the ingredients that helps these companies to extract extraordinary performance from very ordinary people. The other major ingredient, as we shall now see, is the ability to inspire their involvement and commitment.

5 Involvement

'People here are committed because they are proud of what they are doing' – *Sir John Sainsbury*

Without exception, each of our successful companies extracts far more from its employees in terms of personal commitment, dedicated hard work and involvement than the typical British company would think possible. Consider the following examples:

Rocco Forte recently arranged for a group of Trusthouse Forte middle managers to attend a training course run by a well-known management centre. 'The course organizers were astounded at the work capacity of those executives. They had to increase the pace. Our senior managers have a high ability to concentrate.

'My father led by example, working long hours, seven days a week. The other executives simply followed suit. Managers in our company work at the weekends more often than not.'

At MFI calamity struck just two days before the opening of a new store in Glasgow, when the premises were flooded. It could not have been at a worse time of year – the middle of Christmas, with doors due to open to the public the first trading day after the holiday. 'The snow conditions were severe,' recalls an executive, 'with travel very difficult. It took Derek Hunt himself thirteen hours to get there from London. Yet over a hundred volunteers came to help from all levels — managers, electricians, cleaners and warehousemen — from as far away as London and Manchester. No one told them to come. They simply heard the news on the grapevine and made their way as fast and as best they could. Eventually we had so many volunteers we were turning them away because we couldn't find enough for them to do.'

On another occasion, severe snow at York blocked all roads. 'The staff all turned up even though the customers couldn't get there,' says Hunt. 'They sold one coffee table at £9.95!' Snow also caused the collapse of the roof of an MFI store in Wales – company volunteers braved the blizzards to make a repair in four days that outside contractors had estimated would take four weeks.

'I'm frequently amazed by the lengths staff will go to,' admits Hunt. 'In October 1983 we opened a new store in Leeds, the biggest we had ever built. Unthinkingly, I contracted to take a group of institutional investors up to see it on the Monday after the opening. It didn't occur to me that the staff would have been working flat out through a record-breaking Thursday, Friday and Saturday, nor that they had already had to work all hours to get the store ready for the Thursday opening, because the stock was late in being transferred.

'Yet when I arrived with fifteen analysts the store was perfect. The entire staff had been there most of the night on Sunday getting things right. The deputy manager of the store hadn't been home since Wednesday morning.'

At STC a major cable-laying contract ran into trouble, explains an executive, 'when we lost six weeks out of what was already a pretty tight schedule. Some of the worst storms in years damaged our cable-laying ship in the Pacific. Our people worked round the clock, twelve hours on, twelve off. The project manager in charge simply said: 'We are not going to be late.' He organized teams of people to rethink the whole job, using their imaginations and his own to think of ways to cut time out of the programme, for example by doing tasks in parallel, rather than one after the other. I don't think he went to bed in the last two weeks. He finished within twenty-four hours of the contract date.'

This automatic pitching in in a crisis even spreads to suppliers. When a ground-staff strike in the Canary Islands meant that tomatoes would not be delivered to M&S, for example, the British Caledonian cabin crew and pilots loaded them instead. Back in London, the pilot came into one of the London stores to check that 'his' tomatoes were on sale.

When a terrorist bomb blew in the windows of the M&S Marble Arch store at the weekend, no one in the company was particularly surprised that the retailer's shopfitting subcontractor turned up unasked the next day to replace the broken glass and clear up. By Monday morning, when most other stores were just beginning to clear the debris from their premises, M&S was back to normal.

At Bulmer the delivery men are unusually helpful to the shopkeepers, often carrying in the boxes and placing the bottles on the shelves. The practice arose when the sales manager explained to them the importance to the company of having the goods on display rather than stuck in a storeroom. It is not unknown for them to use their initiative and make sure that the Bulmer bottles go in front of rival brands.

At Sainsbury, twenty minutes before the opening of a new store, the entire produce stall suddenly collapsed. 'Everybody pitched in,' says director of branch operations Dennis Males. 'We pulled it all down and made a new display with open boxes. We opened on time, with several staff carrying out the broken fittings before the customers came in. We liked the look of the new arrangement so much we made it a normal part of our layout.

'We also had a run of three separate fires that started in freezer departments. The burnt polystyrene insulation covered everything in thick black smoke. Again, everyone mucked in. The fire happened at the weekend. By Thursday we were open for business again. That taught us that it was possible to do refits very fast. Now it is routine for us to close a store at the weekend and reopen after a refit the following Thursday.'

In none of these cases was there any extra incentive for the people involved (and the word 'involved' is deliberately chosen) to behave as they did. Their salary was the same, there was no immediate promise of bonus or promotion. But they perform beyond the call of duty and their behaviour is seen as exceptional only in degree. These companies *expect* such dedication and by and large they get it.

'During a strike at Manchester airport, two of our directors from London cleaned the floor for four weeks,' recalls one Pritchard manager. 'When a crisis occurs in this company, managers are expected to tell their wives that the job comes first.'

In Search of Excellence identified a strong productivity orientation in the US companies it examined. This is evident in the British companies, and especially so among the companies we surveyed by questionnaire. Among these companies Comet and Blue Circle, for example, both rated themselves as 'outstanding' in what Peters and Waterman describe as 'productivity through people' and Northern Engineering, Sirdar, William Morrison, Laporte and Dalgety all rate themselves well above average.

But many of our very successful companies also show a high *profit* orientation, where managers at least and often the whole work force are well informed about costs and profit and loss, and accord a high priority to profit objectives. In many ways this is a potential advantage for the British company, because it is becoming increasingly clear, both here and in the United States, that concentration on productivity alone can be self-defeating. There is a limit to how much extra productivity can be gained from massaging labour. The pincer of slimmer work forces and shortening working hours have made the gains from making people work harder marginal at best in some industries. In West Germany, in particular, there has been considerable speculation whether in fact the point of maximum efficiency has been passed, to the extent that further tightening of the screws on labour may result in lower productivity.

Traditional approaches to increasing productivity by investment in new technology are also showing cracks. The lesson that higher productive efficiency does not necessarily create higher profits is illustrated by the case of a large confectionery firm. A massive investment programme cut the number of production lines from eighteen to four, while rationalizing the product range and reducing inventories. In the marketplace, however, these individual improvements worked against each other, as the system became too rigid to cope with sudden changes in consumer demand.

By concentrating on profitability rather than productivity, our successful companies have been able to focus employees' attention on how their performance affects the returns from their whole operating unit, rather than just from their own immediate job. In many cases, the employees identify closely with the overall corporate goals; there is a remarkable sharing of objectives as well as values.

So how do these companies obtain such devotion from their employees? It seems there are several common factors that go to make up the involvement perception and these are:

- pride in ownership
- high degree of communication
- high pay and/or incentives
- promotion from within
- stress on training
- recognition of the 'social' side of work
- genuine respect for the individual

Pride in ownership

'Without exception people here are pro Pritchard,' says one of the cleaning company's middle managers. 'I don't find the cynicism here that I've found in other companies I've worked for. Here it's a job and a hobby, too.'

Talk to employees of one of our successful companies and by and large there is an unmistakable air of pride – sometimes even arrogance, admits Maurice Saatchi – in the company they work for. They recognize that there is something special about the organization, something that makes them feel good about being part of it. Some of the elements that make up that feeling are the way they regard top management, the belief that their company is the best in its field, and the acceptance that the company has high standards of goods or services and of general integrity. Somehow the company has earned their respect.

This feeling of pride finds expression in many ways. Malcolm Cotton, managing director of Clark's Ltd, recalls how, not long ago, a small group of production workers at Bath told him bluntly on one of his factory visits that they would not buy the shoes they were making for their own children, and that the styling was inadequate. They were concerned, it transpired, that the company might be letting its high standards slip. Clark's responded swiftly, producing a short video in which the director responsible explained that the company was aware of the problem and had already begun corrective action. The workers who made the original complaint were invited to company headquarters at Street to see for themselves what was being done.

In the older-established companies, the feeling of pride stems partly from the maintenance of at least vestiges of craftsmanship. Bulmer, for example, deliberately retained the traditional varieties of cider when the big brewers were replacing the traditional beers with gas-filled substitutes. Associated Dairies' stores group makes a conscious attempt to retain long-established crafts. Meat is supplied to the butcher's counter primed but not dressed or arranged, so that the butcher can still exercise his craft in presentation. In the same way, the in-store bakeries are encouraged to show off their skills.

Most people find identity during their working lives in the job that they do. Normally people refer to themselves by 'I'm an accountant' – or delivery driver or factory supervisor. In our successful companies people are more likely to describe themselves as 'a deliveryman for Bulmer's', or 'a sales assistant at MFI'. It is the difference between owning an occupation and owning a specific job. Hence our description, 'pride in ownership'.

In addition to the cultural elements that make people feel pride in ownership, there are a number of overt actions that our successful companies have taken to encourage this level of involvement.

One is the obvious route of financial participation via profit-sharing or share ownership schemes. Virtually all our successful companies had installed share ownership schemes or were in the process of doing so. In most cases, they extended right down to the shop floor. A few retailers were obliged to restrict their schemes to managerial and supervisory ranks because of the relatively high proportion of transitory labour in their organizations. The Sainsbury scheme, however, includes part-time employees as well.

Although all the company chairmen had been concerned initially that employees would sell off shares as soon as they could realize their cash value (as happened to ICI employee shares, which were bought from the employees as they left the factory gate), in practice the retention level is very high. Says Marks & Spencer director John Salisse, 'About 35,000 of our staff have shares now. Hardly any of them sell their shares.' M&S staff hang on to their shares because they know they are a good investment.

At Sainsbury many thousands of the employees are shareholders under a scheme that puts 15 per cent of profits over a 2.5 per cent margin into a pot, which has more than trebled in four years. 'One of the reasons we went public was to widen our share ownership,' says Sir John Sainsbury. 'We now have some shop-floor staff with holdings worth around £15,000.'

Says Allied-Lyons chairman Sir Derrick Holden-Brown, 'Our scheme is in two parts: savings-related and straight options. We set aside up to five per cent of the share capital for the issue of options under both parts of the scheme. Some 4000 employees have taken up options and although many of these are the key people, there is a good cross-section of ordinary employees. It is our experience that, when their options mature, the majority of employees hold on to at least some of their shares.'

Clark's, although it is a private company, opened an employee share scheme at the end of the 1970s, to supplement an existing scheme for managers. The scheme is triggered when Clark's exceeds the national industrial average of gross profits to sales turnover. The idea, explains Malcolm Cotton, 'is eventually to give everyone who spends their career here a shareholding roughly worth the house they are living in'.

In some cases, the returns to employees have been spectacular. Managers at Bejam who had made a £30 investment in the company's shares saw their investment turn into £7000 upon flotation.

There are a number of practical advantages to employee shareholdings beyond the sense of involvement they supply. One, expressed by Bulmer, is the fact that a significant employee shareholding helps to protect the company against takeover. Another is that commuting employee bonuses to shares retains cash in the business and reduces the need for external borrowing. But the prime benefit is probably the fact that large numbers of employees will have a genuine interest and an increased understanding of the company's financial position. Bulmer reinforces that understanding with regular reports on share price movements in the company newspaper. Employees receive the employee annual report at home, so their spouses can take an interest too, and attend an employee annual general meeting, where the questions are at least as penetrating as the official annual general meeting the day before. The cider firm is also one of the few British quoted companies to have taken its employee representatives to the Stock Exchange to meet and talk to the jobbing brokers.

It is interesting that companies such as Saatchi & Saatchi which have significant operations in the United States find that share options are a stronger motivator there – hence Saatchi's decision to seek quotations on US exchanges. Saatchi, which was one of the very first companies to take advantage of the British employee share option legislation of the 1970s, was also convinced that, at a senior level at least, the involvement that comes from owning part of the firm makes a major difference in personal commitment. Says Maurice Saatchi: 'Some time ago, we analysed whether companies where the management had a stake did better than companies where they didn't – and they did.'

Another way of developing involvement is an active drawing in of people to practical efforts that go beyond their immediate job. One company has trained delivery men to 'sell' the company as they go around, for example, while parts of Allied-Lyons' brewing division have actively involved the whole spectrum of employees in gaining new custom. For example, Tetley Walker, an Allied-Lyons subsidiary, has increased market share in the free trade area with the help of ordinary employees. When the salesmen pitch for new business at working-men's clubs or leisure centres, they take with them draymen, brewers and a variety of white-collar workers. The personnel manager explains how he can advise the client on industrial relations matters and staffing; the tele-sales staff explain how they take orders and the company surveyor describes how he can help them to get the best value for money out of repairs and extensions. Each of these people makes it clear why getting the club's custom is important to him or her.

Explains Tetley Walker free trade sales director Roger Parker: 'We wanted to put more in front of them than just a salesman with a smart car. We wanted them to see the drayman who makes sure the beer arrives on time and the technical services man who fixes their cellar equipment if things go wrong.'

Apart from gaining the company new business, the all-in approach has helped open the employees' eyes to commercial realities. 'It has shown them that customers are not won over as easily as they supposed,' says Parker.

The broadening of people's exposure to the business they work for is also achieved in some of our companies through project groups made up from people drawn from several levels and departments of the organization, to consider real problems. Several are heavily into quality circles or similar schemes – STC alone has 100 circles in operation.

Very often, however, it is the small incidents that make the difference in making people appreciate the broad implications of what they do. One company with a strong reputation for this is Systime, a computer-based company that grew swiftly in the 1970s. Systime's chief executive Brian Gow placed great emphasis on ensuring people understood what happened to the work they did after it left them. On one occasion, concerned at reports of transit damage to deliveries of expensive hardware to overseas customers, Gow despatched one of the young men in the packing department to the Middle East with instructions to stand at the airport and watch how packing cases were handled. Having seen them bumped, dropped, sat on and left out in the baking sun for days, the young packer came back with a very clear idea of how essential it was that his job was well done. He communicated his experience to other employees in the department. Damage in transit plummeted.

The third comon way our successful companies use to create pride in ownership is by formal or informal schemes of employee participation.

At STC, Alex Park lights up with enthusiasm as he talks of the company's attempts at involving employees at all levels. One particular experiment a few years ago – and well before quality circles became fashionable – was aimed at finding out 'whether everyone in the factory could be involved in using their brain and mind fully, and if they could, would they *want* to be involved?'

The plant chosen for the experiment was Treforest in South Wales, where STC employed 600 people making telephone units. 'It took us two years to get the programme off the ground,' says Cooper. 'We trained the managers in what happens if you have a participative style – what to do if people start to run away with ideas that you know are stupid? Or what do you do if they have no ideas at all?

'One supervisor seemed to be against the scheme. It turned out that he was just unable to talk in front of a group. We asked: "Are there other people with this problem?" When we found there were, we ran a course in public speaking for them.'

The project was introduced by the managers and the trade union representatives together, to emphasize that this was a co-operative venture. Then the employees and managers together selected five areas on which they could concentrate to seek operating improvements. These were revitalizing the suggestion scheme, improving health and safety, reorganizing maintenance, redesigning the test department, and energy conservation.

The results were immediate and dramatic. The value of cost-saving measures (and hence of cash awards to employees) rocketed to four times their previous level, while accidents plummeted by 75 per cent. The employees organized their own fire-fighting team. Real improvements were made in the testing department and in energy conservation and the installation of new maintenance equipment took place without any machine down-time or production losses. Since then, the employees themselves have taken in hand and cured an absenteeism problem. The employee representatives told management they simply hadn't realized how severe the problem was.

STC has also embarked on massive consultation programmes to deal with specific issues, such as the introduction of a new pension scheme. 'We put six cars on the road and sent personnel people to meet everyone in small groups asking them what they thought of the new plan,' recalls Cooper. 'They pointed out that the widow's benefit was not good enough and that the proposals were unfair to part-timers. We incorporated their suggestions. When the union representatives said, "That's not what people want," we were able to prove that it was, from our field reports.'

Every unit of Trusthouse Forte has a consultative committee. The minutes appear on the staff notice board, up to the divisional personnel office, the group personnel office and the divisional managing director. 'It helps us pick up problems early,' says Rocco Forte.

The degree of formal consultation with employees varies from company to company, being negligible in the younger organizations and stronger in the long-established companies. Indeed there seems to be a significant correlation between the extent of formalized employee/management consultation and the age of the company. One of the companies to have taken this to great lengths is Bulmer, which has had a European-style works council since 1977. The council considers all policy matters and decisions that might affect the future of the mass of employees, including the overall statement of company objectives in the annual report. It also has a subcommittee that looks at the impact of new technology, attempting to forecast the implications for employment levels and for specific jobs and arrange retraining well in advance.

However well-meant they may be, employee participation and consultation arrangements can often founder when faced with really difficult and unpalatable decisions, such as large-scale redundancies. But Bulmer's employee council was sufficiently aware of the company's trading position and the need to slim labour that it took over the task of deciding who should go. It also monitored what happened to the redundant workers for eighteen months to ensure that most of them found alternative employment.

United Biscuits, too, has found that its practice of having multitudes of consultative committees to air employee/company problems has eased painful closures. 'We had little problem closing our Osterley factory because everyone understood why,' says one of the company's senior executives. 'Sir Hector was able to walk through the factory the day after the announcement without problem.' Sir Hector has also proposed an employee consultation scheme in which employees who fulfil certain length-of-service criteria should be enfranchised in much the same way as ordinary shareholders. Implementing such a scheme would require a change in Company Law.

STC's employee participation was similarly put to the test when the work force had to be slimmed by one-third. The cause was a sudden slamming on of the brakes on capital expenditure in the telephone service. 'The Government cut back and the Post Office cancelled two years out of our five-year forward order programme. It was a major exercise in consultation all the way,' says Cooper.

'A lot of the managers said, "All this participation is for the birds now, isn't it?" We said, "No, the real test is in the bad times." Consultation doesn't mean asking people to agree their factory should be closed. That's our decision.

'In one case, a factory was to be shut and its production moved to the other end of the country. We said: "You may not agree with our decision, but we will tell you why and how we made it. If you can provide us with new information, or other ways we could tackle the problem, we will see if they can work." They put up lots of alternatives.

'The factory manager complained, "Every time I knock down a suggestion, they come up with another one. When will it end?" After two or three weeks, however, the union representatives agreed that, although they didn't like the decision, it was time to talk about minimizing the social consequences of the closure.'

During the whole of this volatile and traumatic cutback – of some 7000 employees across the country – the company lost only one man-hour per worker through strikes or stoppages. 'The employees knew', says Cooper, 'that while we do care about people, we are absolutely hard-nosed about facts.'

High degree of communication

'Those who have no information can take no responsibility. Those who have information have no choice but to take responsibility,' said Jan Carlsson, chief executive of Scandinavian airline SAS at a conference in London. It is a message which is certainly not lost on our successful companies. They have an armoury of different techniques aimed both at passing information down to those who need it and at listening to what people below have to say. These techniques tend to operate in parallel with the formal reporting and monitoring systems, although there is often considerable cross-over between the two.

In addition to the now almost standard battery of employee annual reports, videos from the chief executive and formal cascade briefing systems, the successful companies encourage communication both through mass gatherings and informal face-to-face encounters.

STC and Racal both have annual meetings of up to a thousand managers where the chairman delivers a state-of-the-company message and answers questions. Racal's meetings are more of a family affair, with wives attending. STC's are more formal, perhaps in part because of memories of less successful attempts at the same sort of thing by one of the four chief executives who preceded Corfield at rapid intervals. That particular chairman called upon a gathering of managers not to be afraid to speak their minds. Within weeks, the first three to speak up had been fired!

The STC gatherings, called Management Information Meetings, are intended to create a cascade effect. Some 1400 people attend, in their own time, to minimize the disruption to work routines. 'If each of them talks to twenty others in the course of the next few weeks we cover the whole company at only second hand,' says Corfield.

'It's almost like a shareholders' meeting. We answer to the employees for the performance over the past year and look forward to the next four years. We account for our stewardship of the business. The climax is a long question-and-answer session. I was advised not to do it, that every barrack-room lawyer would hog the floor.

'In fact, any person who gets up with a view towards embarrassment receives very little encouragement from the rest of the audience, because they want to get to the heart of things.

'Anyone who can't put a question there can put it in writing. All those questions are answered in writing in a report that comes out afterwards.'

These exercises are more than just internal public relations. 'Knowledge is power,' says Corfield. 'When employees learn more from their union representatives than from their management, the power structure is distorted. To communicate is to commit and to commit is to assume responsibility.'

The informal small gathering is central to the day-to-day communication of objectives and culture in AGB, refining and restating to as many as possible in the company the objectives outlined and agreed at the group seminar.

There are monthly lunches with a dozen executives, chosen on rotation so that everyone attends at least once every two years. (Twelve, in Audley's view, is the optimum number for an informal discussion – and also the capacity of the chairman's dining-room.) 'They are semi-structured in that each has a theme,' says Audley. 'They are meant to be hard-hitting and critical, cards-on-the-table affairs.' Overseas directors find such occasions especially valuable.

These 'horizontal' meetings of people at roughly the same level are duplicated further down the organization. There are also vertical lunches, especially for new managers. Audley and a sprinkling of senior managers mingle with potential executives at graduate trainee level and board members of newly acquired or created subsidiaries. 'People take pride in what they have achieved and are right in believing that I want to hear all about it.'

STC's Alex Park has long practised informal briefing lunches with representative groups of employees. 'At the top of our notepaper we have the words "We help people communicate". So we have a lot to live up to. There is no bigger respect you can pay a subordinate than to hear his point of view.

'I have a regular lunch with twelve people, none of them direct subordinates to me. We have a pre-lunch drink, then go through to the main course with social chatter. After that I take over the session, which operates on very simple rules. The first is that in that room we are all equal, expressing a personal point of view. No one is superior to anyone else. The second is that no one can comment on his superiors. The third is that questions are encouraged but that I might not be able to answer some of a commercial nature.

'We talk about the company, its aspirations and their aspirations. We identify blockages in communications and any other problems they bring up.

'There are no reports written. They can tell their colleagues as much or as little as they wish.

'In the past four years there have only been three occasions when someone couldn't come. These lunches are very popular.'

The discussion lasts an hour only. But the reverberations continue for much longer. Many of the people attending have never met before. But encounters over lunch with the division head have a remarkable networking effect. 'I often find when I visit a plant that people there are still in regular contact with other employees they met for the first time around the lunch table,' says Park.

One STC division invited employee representatives to attend its regular management meetings as observers. The union shop stewards responded, when they saw that the offer was genuine, by inviting management to send representatives to the shop stewards' committee meetings. At STC head office there are also informal open evenings where directors meet and talk with people from all levels in the company.

Again, there are examples of good practice in this area from many companies outside our elite selection. Scottish & Newcastle brewery, for example, has achieved a remarkable change in attitudes on the shop floor in recent years. It has a whole series of conventional employee communications such as employee annual reports, but the innovation that has made most difference is a twice-yearly get-together entitled 'The Chairman's Forum'.

The forty attendees at the Chairman's Forum are drawn from all levels and areas within the company, from shop floor to middle management, together with two representatives of each of the trade unions recognized by the company. The atmosphere of these meetings is sharply different from normal management/union encounters. Negotiating and bargaining are mutually banned from the agenda. The objective of the meeting is to examine the realities of S&N's business position in an objective and unthreatening way, without anyone feeling the need to politick or score points.

It works well. The chairman begins the sessions with a review of the state of the company, putting what is happening to S&N into context with events in the markets the company sells to, the overall national and international economic situation, advances in technology and where the company is going. Guest speakers also give papers on issues such as the impact of European legislation. Finally, each meeting takes a different part of the company and analyses its current and future progress in detail. Much of the data is highly confidential, especially where it relates to detailed plans, but there has never been a breach of confidence.

One of the rules of the Chairman's Forum is that any issue can be discussed and that no information will be deliberately withheld. The level of information given frequently exceeds that given to shareholders or investment analysts. The chairman and his colleagues give straight answers to every question.

The effect of these meetings, as they have gradually been accepted into the normal ways of doing things at S&N, has been an acceptance throughout the company of the need to slim down and to abandon restrictive practices. The forty participants, who change from one forum to the next, act as opinion-formers, passing on their understanding of commercial realities. Significantly, the union representatives are as enthusiastic as management about the scheme.

At an operating level, MFI's area managers hold an 'open forum' in each of the stores under their control every month. Attending are representatives of all the job categories in the store, such as salesman, cleaner and warehouseman. The objective is to allow staff to ask questions and make observations about any aspect of the company's operations in a relaxed atmosphere. The minutes of the meetings work their way up from the area manager through the operations manager and regional manager and finally to the retail operations director, who sits on the board. He brings up at board meetings any issues which are particularly serious or which seem to be emerging in a definable pattern.

Written communications, while never as convincing as face-to-face meetings, are none the less important in our sample companies. At STC, Corfield and his fellow directors each receive hundreds of letters from employees and pensioners every year. Each is answered personally, as a matter of respect for the individual. 'Yes, it's a chore. But it does away with the Dear Sir, Thank you for your letter, yours faithfully syndrome,' says Corfield.

But just how deeply into the culture of these organizations has this passion for disclosure of information penetrated? At first sight, it could be concluded that employee communications is merely a late-twentieth-century fad. Certainly, in many of our companies, it is a relatively recent phenomenon. At Bulmer, for example, the new finance director found on his arrival in the 1960s that even the chief accountant had never seen the full accounts. One of the first actions of the new team of professionals who took over the day-to-day running of the company was to begin to open up the flow of information, as a means of *changing* the culture. That, too, is a major part of the approach of John Beckett at F.W. Woolworth, who has put the ailing stores chain firmly on to the recovery path.

And that, perhaps, is the difference between our successful companies' perception of communications and that of many less successful companies. A living culture adjusts and assimilates new ideas; it learns from its experiences and develops new responses to new situations. This process can be seen at its clearest in the family-dominated companies, where success seems to be closely tied to the art of keeping the best of traditional values while seeking new values appropriate to the changed times.

So open communications is simply a positive response by adaptive company cultures to a change in the external environment. In our examination of the less successful companies, in Chapter 11, we find in contrast that less successful companies frequently have failed to make this adaptation, even though they may, like for example British Steel, have all the formal trappings of communications media and participative structures.

73

A similar distinction may well apply between successful and unsuccessful young companies, although we have not carried out any comparative research in this area. Certainly, companies such as MFI or Pritchard thrive on transparency of information. At MFI the weekly profit and loss account for each branch is pinned on the staff notice board for all to see. Pritchard allows any employee, at any level, access to the file on any cleaning contract. Says a Pritchard middle manager: 'No one asks why they want the information; it is just taken on trust that they have a good reason.'

High pay and/or incentives

Our successful companies tend to be among the highest payers in their industry sectors. This is not because, being successful, they can afford to pay well. It is rather a matter of a recognition that one way to attract the best people is to offer the best rewards. In some cases these rewards can be very high – witness the £500,000 salary of BOC's Richard Giordano.

'There is', says STC's Corfield with atypical understatement, 'no special merit in a low-wage economy.' The successful companies can often keep the people they want even if they pay below average, simply because of the nature of their working environment, but they see a sharing of rewards as a natural outcome of the creation of wealth. It becomes a self-fulfilling cycle – from involvement, through commitment, greater productivity and profitability, to higher rewards, which increase involvement once more.

Several of the exceptions in our sample pay average or below-average salaries in positions that do not greatly influence the bottom line, but reward well those in key positions. On the other hand, a few are not exceptional payers at executive level. 'A lot of people may not be motivated by more money,' says GEC's Lord Weinstock.

Although they place much higher reliance on other motivating factors than on tapping people's natural aspirations to seek measurable reward in return for effort, these companies would agree with the rest of the sample that low pay is not a viable method of solving problems of competition. They recognize that management's credibility cannot be sustained if employees are expected to sacrifice rewards in hard times, only to be denied a share in the rewards in better times.

This attitude seems to be borne out by a recent international study of work values in six countries – Britain, the United States, Japan, West Germany, Sweden and Israel. The study attempted to identify people's attitudes to work and what affected those attitudes. One conclusion across international barriers was that, while the work ethic was still fairly strong in most countries, companies failed to capitalize on it. (British workers scored lowest of all on the work ethic.) Another conclusion was that the low pay levels in British companies encouraged employees to have low expectations of the rewards for their work.

In the report on the British section of the survey, researcher Paul Sparrow explains: 'The more highly educated were least committed. This is true for West Germany and Sweden as well. The majority of highly educated people worked for material success, and in this they were least likely to be satisfied in their work.' Fortunately, some of this ground was made up by those highly educated people for whom personal fulfilment was more important than material reward. These people, Sparrow found, were more likely to get what they wanted out of work, and hence tended to be among the most committed. In other words, failure to pay well means that a company may be forced to rely for its most motivated leaders on people for whom money is a secondary consideration.

In addition to pay, many of the companies also put great emphasis on an incentive element. The staff at MFI stores, for example, are all – from cleaners to salespersons – covered by a branch incentive scheme. Hence the keen interest taken every Monday morning when the weekly profit and loss account is posted.

Alongside MFI's profit-related bonuses are various incentives related to areas where top management feels a sharper edge is needed. When the issue was customer service each store was scored by an outside agency on its response to a succession of specially primed customers with out-of-the-ordinary or difficult requests and telephone complaints. Each of the company's twenty-four administrative areas can award a prize to the best store in its jurisdiction. The two best stores in the country get to send their entire staff and spouses on an expenses-paid long weekend overseas. Several of MFI's suppliers have adopted similar incentives for units that produce the most consistently high quality.

The trip not only gives the branches something extra to work towards, but provides yet another opportunity for top management and ordinary employees to meet in informal, unthreatening circumstances. The first

75

of these incentive programmes was on raising turnover and took the staff of two stores to Monte Carlo. Hunt and a young warehouseman of twenty-two were the only ones who did not take a partner. 'This young man decided to look after the guv'nor,' recalls another director. 'When Keith missed the coach outing on the second day, after a very jolly night, the warehouseman stayed behind to make sure he was all right.'

At Pritchard, says a junior executive, 'We have extraordinarily good incentive schemes, usually running to at least one-third of salary.'

Housebuilders Barratt Developments also relate incentives to profit-centre performance. All employees share in the profits of their local subsidiary, with directors receiving up to 50 per cent of their remuneration in the form of profit-related bonuses.

Saatchi divides its incentives into two. Profit-related bonuses are distributed as cash or shares, as the employee prefers. There are also spot bonuses, paid out for achieving budget early. The unit chief executive decides how the bonus will be split up between his subordinates. 'There is a strong correlation between quality of performance and what people are paid,' says corporate development manager Simon Mellor. 'If people are not so good, their pay lags. On the other hand, we use salary to try to tie in the people we want to keep.'

Most of these companies have stuck to merit-based remuneration over the past decade even though the majority of British companies have allowed their merit systems to decay. This, considers Peter Brown of Reward Regional Surveys, is probably a significant reason for their superior profit performance. Explains Brown: 'The annual cash increment can be an important motivator, but it has been devalued in many companies. Before inflation, if you got a rise, it was because you were good. Now everyone gets a rise, just to keep up with inflation. Performance differentials between people in management levels are often not rewarded at all. At the same time, many British companies, in order to overcome bargaining restrictions, put in bonus schemes with un-achievable targets. If they failed to pay out three times in a row, they became boomerangs rather than bonuses.'

Brown believes the problem goes much deeper than an enforced response to inflation, however. Its real roots lie in the inability of most companies to assess performance accurately. Even if the company has a system of regular performance appraisal, 'Most managers are unwilling to discriminate. They won't admit the very good or the really bad among their subordinates,' he declares.

'We have to get back to merit as the basis for annual increments,' he continues. 'The evidence we have suggests that the most profitable companies have face-to-face discussions about performance with individual managers and a fair amount of discrimination about how much each person gets.'

A hard-nosed, objective approach to incentive payments certainly seems to be the rule among our successful companies. Hanson Trust's Peter Harper describes his company's practice in this way: 'Assessment of management performance depends on your ability to produce increasing profitability year on year. It is harsh because there are times when the business climate is bad. But it is objective. We couldn't care less what people are. If they can improve profitability year after year they are good men. If they can't get profit up, they aim to get capital employed down so the profitability still rises.

'Any other form of assessment is subjective. Incentive schemes have to be geared to exact profitability, otherwise it just comes down to whether he's a nice fellow or not. Most bonus schemes in the end, if you don't quantify them, come down to whether you like the man's eyes.'

And the formula seems to work within turn-arounds too. One signal example is the change in fortunes at the Imperial Group under Geoffrey Kent. Kent produced an increase in profits of 84 per cent and a growth in return on assets of 65 per cent within two and a half years with a strategy that gave prominence to high rewards for exceptional profit performance. 'I set managers stretching targets,' he told the *Observer*. Once they meet and exceed their targets the cash rewards are substantial. Kent himself is on a performance-related bonus that gives him every reason to encourage line managers to beat their targets.

Promotion from within

Every one of our successful companies puts considerable emphasis on promotion from within. 'All our operational managers come up from the shop floor,' says Rocco Forte. Even in those companies such as Plessey and Bulmer, which have undergone a major cultural change, external appointments at senior level are the exception rather than the rule.

There seem to be three basic reasons, or rationalizations, for this. The first is because, as the industry leader, these companies often see themselves as the harbour of best practice anyway; therefore the talent that they need is most likely to be found within. 'There's a one-way flow of people from us to other contractors,' says Pritchard manager David Openshaw. 'None of them ever come here.'

The second reason is that outsiders do not easily adapt to their culture when plugged in at senior level. One manager at Sainsbury, for example, refers to his first few months in the company as 'a major culture shock'. The third reason is because they see promotion from within as a means of keeping the people they want, of extending the 'family' concept. 'We want anyone with the ambition and ability to feel they can become a managing director in our company,' says Racal's Harrison. 'Everyone here knows their superiors are talent spotters,' adds Bejam's Perry.

STC, where 83 per cent of promotions are from within, has a scheme called Jobscan, listing all the dozens of professional and managerial vacancies. Managers are obliged to allow subordinates to apply and are required not to make obstacles that will hold people down just because they are valuable and difficult to replace where they are. It still makes sure that some senior appointments are from outside, however, to ensure that the company culture does not become excessively inbred.

The practicality of large-scale promotion from within rests to a certain extent on how strong employee involvement is within the corporate culture. Mike Jones, personnel director of Bejam, expresses is succinctly: 'How do you identify talent and potential if you have not got people involved in the company?' he asks.

Plessey, for example, found that it was obliged to go outside for managerial talent in the early 1970s and has been struggling to push up the percentage of internal promotions ever since. 'Ten years ago 70 per cent of our senior appointments were from outside,' says executive director Parry Rogers. 'Now it's 30 per cent and it will be down to 10 or 15 per cent in three years' time.' The change has had a radical effect on turnover among professional staff and managers; in the early 1970s 50 per cent of graduates recruited each year would have quit or been fired within two years, now it takes twice as long. There is still some way to catch up with Rogers' old employers, IBM, where the period is five years. This is probably as far as most companies would want to go in hanging on to staff anyway – beyond that there may develop an unhealthy hanging on of people the company would normally want to get rid of.

Training

If promotion is to come primarily from within, then the onus of management development has to fall internally. All the companies in our survey spend large sums on training every year. Most have extensive courses on everything from technical to human relations skills. But discussion with senior management soon reveals that formal training is seen simply as a reinforcement for the central planks of managerial growth – mentorship and practical experience.

In these companies every manager is a teacher. 'It's very important that people make themselves redundant by bringing on people below them,' says Maurice Saatchi. 'That means they have to feel secure themselves, which means the company has to keep growing.'

In the decentralized companies, training tends to be delegated as far down the line as possible, so that managers will take the responsibility for developing the people below them. In younger companies such as Barratt there is no central personnel or training function, so line managers cannot push the responsibility off on to a staff department. Particularly in the centralized companies, such as Sainsbury or Marks & Spencer, development of subordinates is a significant part of the annual appraisal process. This may not affect the manager's bonus directly, but it plays an important role in determining his eligibility for future promotion. Promotion for those who demonstrate mastery of successive jobs can be swift.

The mentoring philosophy, of nurturing the talents of tomorrow's potential top managers, is impressed down the line by the example of the chief executive and his senior colleagues. BOC's Giordano describes his main role in terms of bringing out the talents of his top 200 managers. Grand Metropolitan's Grinstead uses the regular one-on-one meetings with operational managers behind closed doors to push, cajole and encourage them to develop increased managerial ability – and expects them to do the same down the line. 'It's by face-to-face contact that we communicate our expectations and standards,' he explains. Trafalgar House managing director Eric Parker takes personal responsibility for selection for all key posts – managers who bring on subordinates well have the satisfaction of registering their own Brownie points right at the top. Other, more visible top managers spend hours simply sitting and talking with younger managers, advising them, getting to know them and giving them direction.

Experience, claim several of our successful companies, is still the best teacher of all. In Chapter 2 we saw how some companies deliberately exposed young managers to real problems and responsibilities as early as possible to ensure a swift grounding in leadership, and this applies to all the other managerial skills as well. Pritchard, for example, is noted for its willingness to take on cleaning contracts that other large companies in the business would consider too small to bother with. The reason is at least partly that these contracts provide ideal training grounds for inexperienced managers, where they can make and learn from their mistakes without the risk of major embarrassment or financial loss. At Trafalgar House, says Broackes, 'Young managers can have responsibility showered on them.' Right through the organization even relatively junior managers have the chance to direct their own business unit from a seat on the board of a subsidiary company, trading under its own name. Broackes believes this encourages them to be independent and entrepreneurial, to take responsibility, to control as well as execute. Says a company spokesman: 'In short, we believe in directors.'

The combination of internal promotion and strong emphasis on management development can be a two-edged sword unless the swift pace of growth can be maintained. Failure to grow can force an exodus of talent and widespread frustration. Often the danger of that in itself is enough to keep top management on its toes looking for new fields to conquer. Explains one senior manager at BTR: 'We have grown all our talent internally. Prior to the Thomas Tilling acquisition we were getting to the embarrassing point where we had a surplus of first-class managers seeking a challenge. We learned we had secured Tilling on a Thursday. By the following Monday we were able to start twenty managers in Tilling operations across the world from the United States to Tokyo.'

The strong belief in training pays off in other ways, too. Like most other electronics companies, STC has had to change the structure of its work force radically. But by planning ahead and providing retraining opportunities it has been able to re-employ all but 3 per cent of the people whose jobs have been made technologically redundant. The job security that provides has manifest benefits in employee motivation terms, the company claims.

United Biscuits' Robert Clark asserts that his company's investment in a strong management development programme is quite simply because 'they are the leaders of tomorrow'.

Recognition of the 'social' side of work

This isn't the place to wax philosophical about job satisfaction. But one of the ways in which our sample of companies stands out is in the sheer enjoyment employees, especially at management level, get out of even routine work.

'We see humour in everything,' says Bejam's Perry. 'We try to get people as excited by their jobs as they were by football teams as kids.' Tough chief executives with reputations for fine-grinding business opponents talk openly about the 'family atmosphere' of their operations. Allied-Lyons even calls its headquarters employee magazine *Our House*.

Some of our companies enter with equal zest upon an extensive social life outside office hours. In the main these are companies still in their relative youth. The aggressive, hectic nature of work in a company that is growing fast seems to demand some form of explosive release. Racal, for example, has at least thirty major social events across the company each year. At the main managerial get-together, held each year in a London hotel, the audience is asked to place bets on the identity of the mystery top-line entertainer. The winning table chooses the charity to which the pool will go.

The event is meant to show top management letting its hair down; and it does. Similarly, on the occasion of the Racal agents' banquet at Racalex 82 (claimed to be the largest private exhibition of its kind in the world) two camels were brought into the dining-room and Harrison, who had had no forewarning, was asked and agreed to ride round the hall, dressed as a jockey and hanging on as best he could.

Harrison had little choice but to take the joke; he has a reputation within the company as a man who plays as well as works hard. 'He has often sent people off to Heathrow on mythical trips or to meet non-existent visitors,' says a colleague.

MFI maintains a similar giddy social round, with Hunt and his fellow directors often up till the small hours with small groupings of branch managers. MFI also has the same impish appreciation of a good prank, as witnessed by its reaction to the bill from its merchant bank for a rights issue. Over lunch with the bankers one of the MFI directors surreptitiously ran the Jolly Roger up the bank's flagpole. The bank had the good humour to leave it there for twenty-four hours before telexing back: 'After a gallant resistance, the flag was finally struck at twelve noon!'

The zest with which Hunt and his colleagues throw themselves into these social contacts with other employees would exhaust most other executive teams. The directors even challenge other ranks to an annual football match. (Hunt broke his nose in one.)

At Asda tales abound of bizarre events that result from collegial celebrations. A manager recalls the following incidents:

'There was the never-to-be forgotten moment when, at a new store opening, the managing director, the board, the VIPs and hundreds of customers were poised at nine a.m. with burning expectation for the doors to open. The only person missing was the assistant store manager. He was still blissfully sleeping off the previous night's celebrations.

'On another occasion, the managing director "persuaded" a fully clothed controller to take an unexpected swim in the swimming pool of the Aberdeen Sheraton Hotel.'

Usually these pranks occur outside of normal working hours. But one incident recently involved an assistant store manager wandering around the city centre asking policemen and passers-by if they had seen his 200 missing staff. In true participative spirit, he had permitted the staff to choose for themselves where to assemble in the event of a bomb scare. He had forgotten to ask them the location, which turned out to be a local hostelry.

The schoolboy atmosphere in these companies is strongly reminiscent of Japanese companies, where evening carousals have traditionally been part of the cementing of the managerial team. The typical British management team, by contrast, is an artificial affair, which breaks up at the end of the working day and reassembles the next morning; social events with other ranks are awkward, forced affiairs uncomfortable to all concerned.

Employees respond to this kind of relaxed and jovial togetherness – as long as they perceive it to be genuine – with their own pranks. 'We take the piss mercilessly out of our directors,' says an MFI middle manager. Bulmer's employees gave former chief executive Peter Prior his own trolley because of his habit of pitching in if he saw a large load in need of shifting. 'How many other work forces would have had the confidence to do that?' asks one of the managers.

Bejam's directors also spend a great deal of time socializing. But the external social life is seen as a reward for performance and may be withheld if targets are not achieved. Says Perry: 'We had a low growth in 1983, so we are not holding a celebration party. What's to celebrate? People accepted it well, because they knew the party would be back in

1984 and because they understood the fairness of it. I don't believe in meaningless pats on the back.'

One impact of this giddy social round is that people who can't stand their working colleagues socially move on, so the team becomes tighter. It is also more difficult to sustain organizational politics in such an environment.

At the same time, it has to be admitted that a prerequisite is a long-suffering spouse who accepts that the job comes first; and that many people find obligatory carousals and horseplay thoroughly frightful!

Genuine respect for the individual

There is no doubt that our successful companies can be ruthless in achieving business goals, although as we shall see later, they tend to have higher-than-average ethical standards. But their ability to act decisively in business crises is matched in most cases by an instinctive reaction to personal crises. Marks & Spencer director John Salisse describes his company as 'highly disciplined but caring'. Part of the respect such organizations have for people automatically implies that the company will respond generously to genuine need.

As a result, the mythology of many of our successful companies contains substantially true stories of notable acts of generosity. United Biscuits, for example, bought a kidney machine for an employee whose wife needed it and could not obtain one through the National Health Service. One of the few things which really upsets Sir Hector Laing is if he is not informed when an employee or a member of his or her family is seriously ill. Factory directors take their cue from this and ensure that such cases are dealt with considerately in their own area.

On occasion, United Biscuits' concern for the welfare of its employees goes beyond what they are prepared for. In 1978, for example, Laing offered job security if the employees pursued a wage policy that allowed the company to reinvest 20 per cent of added value back into the business. The idea was not accepted as a basis for negotiation.

Marks & Spencer is often regarded as the most welfare-oriented company in Britain. But this aspect of the firm is really just a deeper reflection of the same paternalism that runs through most of our successful companies. Indeed, it could be said that paternalism is far from dead; it has merely metamorphosed into a form more acceptable to the late twentieth century. Instead of being a matter of part guilt, part philanthropic concern by comfortably-off Victorian gentlemen, paternalism has become a practical response to the need to create a positive working environment. Benefits are no longer imposed upon employees, but offered whenever a need becomes apparent.

Salisse dismisses the £50 million the company spends each year on employee benefits and welfare as a fleabite in comparison to the returns. 'Just look at our profit figures,' he says, shrugging his shoulders. The broad range of benefits, from non-contributory pensions to free breast screening pay back in a variety of ways, including staff turnover considerably lower than in most other high street stores.

The company's concern for the people it employs goes back to the earliest days of the establishment of its culture. But many of the key innovations date from the middle of this century, from simple observation by directors of how the staff worked and lived. Said the current Lord Sieff in 1983: 'Many managers do not appreciate the conditions under which their fellow employees work and some don't even know. Management cannot know what conditions are like unless they frequently visit the shop floor and make use of the amenities which are provided for staff; if they are not good enough for management they are not good enough for anybody.

'At Marks & Spencer we are continuously involved with the wellbeing and progress of our 45,000 staff. We treat everyone as an individual. We have over 900 people in our personnel department, mainly working throughout the stores, as part of the store management team. Each staff manager is responsible for the welfare, training and progress of the fifty or sixty people in her or his care.

'We delegate responsibility to local managers with a guideline to deal with human problems quickly. We say: "If you are going to make a mistake when dealing with human beings, ensure that you err on the side of generosity." This is rarely abused.'

One of the first benefits introduced by M&S was a high calibre of staff canteen, now commonplace across British business. Simon Marks and Israel Sieff introduced the canteens during the depression, when discussions with a salesgirl who looked unwell in their Kilburn store revealed that she was going hungry during the day. She was the only breadwinner in her family, because both her brothers and her father were out of work, so every penny went home. M&S's response was to ensure that everyone who worked for the company could buy a good three-course meal for about the price of a sandwich. The price of meals was kept at six old pence for forty years. When the decision was finally taken to raise the price, says Sieff, it was one of the most heated board meetings in the history of the company. Before the National Health Service was introduced M&S also arranged for doctors, dentists and chiropodists to visit the stores at regular intervals. It was not entirely philanthropic; it ensured that they spent the time at work they would otherwise have needed to spend in crowded surgery waiting rooms.

M&S, over the years, also put pressure on its suppliers to adopt similar welfare schemes, and many have done so. Among the inducements is the assistance of M&S's own specialist staff to help them in the design of canteen layout, pension schemes or health programmes. This pressure arose because Simon Marks needed to answer the call of nature while visiting the construction site of a new store. Sieff tells the story himself: 'About 1955 I was visiting stores with Simon Marks. We were leaving the Dartford store, which was in the middle of a major rebuilding programme which would take nearly two years. The rain was pouring down; as we got into the car Simon said to me: "I must go to the gents." Instead of going back into the store he went to the building labourers' area where the workers were sitting under a tarpaulin slung over two girders from which the rain was coming down in buckets, drinking mugs of tea, eating thick sandwiches and looking as miserable as hell. The toilet was a primitive closet. In the car Simon said, I remember it well: 'You know, Marcus, those fellows will be working on that site for one to two years. They are really working for us; we can't have two different standards."

'Next day we suggested to the then heads of Bovis, who were the builders, that between us we had to do better. It was agreed that on every job the first structures to go up would be decent facilities for the workers – canteen, proper lavatories and shower, drying room for clothes. In the last twenty-seven years Bovis, who do 95 per cent of our building, have completed about 400 major jobs for us, costing hundreds of millions of pounds, and with one exception no building has been delivered a day late, but many handed over weeks early. And Bovis are profitable, progressive and held in high respect. This philosophy of looking after people is widespread among and implemented by our suppliers.'

Perhaps the most poignant story of M&S's approach to the welfare of its staff is that of Esther Brown, one of the first sales assistants on Michael Marks' original stall. Esther eventually became manageress of one of the company's stores, a job she held until 1911. There was no further contact from her for fifty years, then suddenly in the mid 1960s the welfare department received a telephone call from a Manchester hospital. An old lady had come round from a serious operation and in her delirium was repeating over and over again, 'Mr Marks and Mr Sieff would help me, if only they knew.' Once Esther had been identified, the company purchased her a small house and awarded her a pension.

Esther's tale is not unusual within M&S. Sieff reads out a letter he has just received from the widower of a recently deceased employee. The letter speaks of how the M&S staff visited her regularly in hospital over a long period of recurring cancer and how the local store bought flowers for twenty hospital staff who had cared for her during her illness. The widower was also allocated his wife's pension.

'Whatever we have done because we felt we had a moral obligation, turned out to be good for business within five years,' says Sieff.

While they may not go to such extremes as M&S, most of our successful companies do practise a strong respect for the individual and for what they feel is right in terms of dealing with human problems. Again, the example frequently comes from the top. STC's Corfield recalls how, on one occasion early after his appointment, he had to intervene in the punishment of a manager who had abused the trust placed in him. The manager concerned had persistently defrauded the company over a period of years on his expense account. 'A very good director felt that the long service the man had enjoyed meant that we could not bring in the law, although the man would have to be discharged, with the loss of his pension. I asked the director to reconsider, taking account that, if the company took the law into its own hands, it must be absolutely sure the penalty would not be greater than the law would have imposed. It took me several weeks to convince him that I was right and that the man should retain his pension rights.

'I don't think any current director would even think of taking such harsh action against an individual now. The culture that has grown up simply wouldn't allow it.'

Summary

The involvement factor gives our successful companies a view on individuals that instinctively draws them them into something greater than themselves. Sainsbury's Dennis Males tells new graduate recruits at their induction that they must become committed to the company. If they fail to do so they will not adapt to the culture and will neither contribute to nor enjoy company life, he explains.

Involvement cannot exist on its own; it is integrally bound up with the company's perceptions of integrity, of leadership and of individual autonomy. Although a few companies have said, 'We will create involvement by our people' and have subsequently done so, in most of our companies the sense of involvement has developed of its own accord, because it seemed right and fitted in with the rest of the company's way of doing things. It is not difficult to think of major corporations, in Britain and elsewhere, which have the same stated desire to involve employees at all levels, yet have manifestly failed to do so, in spite of using many of the same techniques and communications methods as our sample of successful companies. The reason, we suggest, may be that involvement only occurs *en masse* when employees identify with the overall culture of the company.

6 Market orientation

'Most of our most successful managers are people who spend most of their time attending to the customers' – *Peter Pritchard*

To say that 'the customer is king' is an understatement for many of our successful companies. For them, good customer relations and a deep understanding of the market in which they operate are essential, routine and unquestioned parts of their day-to-day method of doing business.

The reputation of Marks & Spencer for taking back goods from dissatisfied customers without question is exemplary, but not particularly unusual among our success sample. (Though it is unlikely that anyone else is used quite so widely as an oblique means of cashing cheques on a Saturday afternoon.) Racal, for example, responds to customer problems by flying out an engineer immediately and without argument. Occasionally the journey proves unnecessary, as when an engineer rushed out to investigate an equipment failure in Nigeria, only to find that it had not been turned on. Company policy is to sort out the problem first, then look into who is responsible. In most cases, Racal makes no charge.

Such generosity is, however, much easier to support when you are making large profits than when you are operating on thin margins, admits Harrison.

While not all the companies go to such extremes, they all have a very strong perception about how they fit into their marketplace and how they should interrelate with the customer. This finds expression in several ways, including the following:

- maintenance of brand strength
- swift and comprehensive dealing with complaints
- emphasis on quality control
- hunger for market information
- market-oriented research and development

Maintenance of brand strength

Clark's, says Daniel Clark, is all about brands. The company puts tremendous effort into developing and maintaining the Clark's name. So much so that one firm of consultants, advising the company on diversification, claimed that they could put the name Clark to almost anything and it would sell. 'We have to maintain the integrity of our brands,' says Clark. 'We want them to be there in fifty years' time.' Research has shown Clark's brand to be a remarkable seven times stronger than its nearest competitor.

The public belief in the quality and reliability of Clark's sometimes goes to absurd lengths. Cases are common of customers coming into retailers with shoes five years old or more and complaining that they have worn out. They had assumed that Clark's shoes lasted forever.

Clark's feels that marketing and promoting the brand is so important it cannot be left to staff functionaries. 'We don't have any marketing eunuchs here' is a catchphrase that frequently echoes around Street. Instead, marketing is incorporated into much larger jobs among a much wider range of people.

High spending on brand promotion is now an accepted characteristic of the brewing industry. The first brewing company to realize the possibilities of national beer brands was Allied-Lyons' beer division, which now invests heavily in the promotion of both national and local brands. It requires an act of faith, maintains managing director Douglas Strachan, because the benefits of promotional spending now are often not seen for five to seven years.

Bulmer takes a very similar attitude, investing heavily in brand promotion even when times are tough and the instinctive reaction is to cut back on overheads and non-essentials. Convincing employees that this makes good business sense can be difficult when you are laying people off, admits Nelson, but 'Without our brands we are not a company.'

Few of the more recently established companies have seized upon the benefits of strong brand identification more strongly than Barratt. Sir Lawrie Barratt 'sells and builds rather than builds and sells'. The first housebuilder ever to advertise on British television, he created a national brand awareness through the twin symbols of the helicopter and the oak tree.

Barratt demonstrates a closeness to the market that would do more than justice to most consumer goods manufacturers. Indeed, his whole approach treats homes as another form of consumer product. It begins with the concept that home-buying is a complex, troublesome and expensive business and that good marketing should 'make home-buying easy'.

To do that, Barratt has progressively introduced a whole range of services that take the hassle out of house purchase. For first-time buyers, it offers 100 per cent mortgages or help with saving up the deposit, full fixtures, fittings and basic white goods within the purchase price, and deferred payments. For people who already own homes, it arranges to buy the old property, making it one of the largest dealers in second-hand homes in the country. At any one time, Barratt holds a stock of about 700 houses, many of which it will do up before reselling, to increase the resale price. Sir Lawrie talks of customers being able to move in with 'only a toothbrush and a light bulb'.

Every foreseeable eventuality that might reduce the volume of home sales is covered by meticulous planning. 'If the mortgage rate goes up, other builders cut back on sites. We just have to push a button and bring out a new purchase plan,' says Sir Lawrie. Responsiveness to the market has led to a constant stream of innovations, from special units for re-tirees to studio apartments for young singles. 'We are always looking for new market niches,' says Sir Lawrie.

The success of this intensive marketing approach can be seen not just in the rapid growth of the company, from sales of £32 million in 1974 to £512 million in 1983, but in the fact that other national builders have been obliged to follow suit.

The sound of coconut salesmen on Spanish beaches calling out that their wares are on offer 'at Asda prices' is music to Noel Stockdale's ears. But few companies can match the item of folklore concerning the telephone call Lord Sieff's father is said to have received from a high-ranking Vatican official. 'A number of saints are being demoted,' said the official. 'But you may rest assured that St Michael remains untouched.'

Brand strength is closely allied to market leadership, which most of our successful companies seek actively in all the sectors where they operate. The fact that the selection process for this project used market leadership as a criterion means that we cannot draw conclusions here, other than that all the successful companies perceive the achievement of market leadership as important.

Swift and comprehensive dealing with customer complaints

'A client in the City complained one Friday recently,' recalls Pritchard manager David Openshaw. 'No less than eight senior managers, including the managing director, turned up over the weekend, to make sure it was put right before Monday morning.'

Topheavy it may seem, but this level of reaction is far from unusual at Pritchard. Customer service starts with regular visits to each customer by the local manager or his assistant. The head office switchboard opens at six a.m. so that any complaints can be responded to immediately. Usually the company aims to have the local manager or the contract supervisor on the spot by the time the client opens his offices. Within twenty-four hours the client is visited by the branch manager or regional manager. The more serious the complaint, the higher the level of management that turns up to sort it out.

The obvious importance the company attaches to ensuring the customer is satisfied pays off in contract renewals. On average cleaning contract customers stay with Pritchard eight to ten years.

Rocco Forte sees all complaints that come to company headquarters and follows them up personally with the head of the division concerned. If the complaint is serious, he insists on seeing the report of the investigation and what has been done to satisfy the customer.

Bejam, which had a somewhat rough-and-ready reputation for complaints handling in its early days, now claims that all complaints are dealt with in twenty-four hours. 'Anyone who complains in writing gets a detailed response,' says finance director John Edwards. 'We contact the customer and we insist the supplier does too.' All complaints are logged and fed into a computer at headquarters, where they are related to products and volume of sales. The computer program also identifies the buyer, giving him the ammunition to put pressure on the supplier. A quality control lab also ensures that every load of a food product that does not have a major national brand behind it is tested before it reaches the shops. Major brands, once accepted, are presumed to be adequately tested by the supplier, until proven otherwise.

Emphasis on quality control

It was Clark's health ethos that led it to initiate its famous foot-gauge. All the quality controls applied in the factory and in delivery to the retail outlets were useless if the customer was sold the wrong pair of shoes. While some quality control could be exercised in Clark's own shops, the only way to ensure that every customer received shoes that really fitted was to persuade every retailer stocking the company's shoes to follow the same practice in measuring for length and width. Providing free training to thousands of people who are not company employees is an expensive business. But it strengthens the brand recognition of Clark's as a manufacturer people can rely upon for well-fitting shoes.

'The key is the belief we are here to stay,' explains John Clothier. 'There's always a temptation to go for the short term and pack customers through. But quality, style, comfort and fit are the things that count in shoe retail, and what determines whether you make money in the long term is how consistently you deliver all of these.'

Marks & Spencer's insistence on quality control is legendary. Says Sieff: 'If it's not good enough for me and my family to eat or wear, it's not good enough to sell.' If is often extremely difficult to detect the fault in goods that the Marks & Spencer buyers have rejected. That was not always the case. The accent on quality is something which has developed over the years and was assimilated into the company culture with relative ease, because of the strong relationship M&S already had with its suppliers. Its strong involvement – some would say interference – in its suppliers' operations was first intended to ensure that they produced what it perceived as the market demand. 'We were the first to tell manufacturers to make what the customer wanted instead of simply buying what they made,' says Salisse. Once established, this relationship was a ready-made vehicle for imposing standards of production and production procedures.

M&S maintains a team of inspectors who visit suppliers' premises, ensuring that quality levels are maintained and making suggestions for improvements. It calculates that a one per cent reduction in faulty merchandise more than pays for all the support services it provides suppliers, including substantial help in areas of employee welfare. M&S reasons that good working conditions are a prerequisite for high-quality production. It lays particular stress on canteens, morale and hygiene, and provides free courses for suppliers on a whole range of employee welfare issues. A regular newsletter keeps suppliers up to date on developments that might improve quality directly or through employee motivation.

'All our long-term suppliers are very profitable,' claims Sieff, suggesting that that is a result of adopting M&S-style management.

Suppliers who do not fall in line, fall out. A large meat supplier, for example, had very poor working conditions for its employees. 'Our business with them was increasing considerably. But they had appalling canteens and lavatories and some of the walls were running with damp. I said I would give them three months to put it right. When I came back there was no improvement. They said, "You'll never stop doing business with us." One month later we gave them two weeks' notice.'

Sainsbury does not usually become so heavily involved in the internal affairs of its suppliers – except in the case of bacon, where, says Sir John, 'We modernized the industry because we couldn't get what we wanted from the suppliers' – but it does take quality control very seriously. Every product that finds its way on to the shelves (there are more than 9000 different items in a typical new store now, with a constant flow of additions and changes) goes to the chairman's committee for approval. 'How many other chairmen have every product they sell pass across their desk?' he asks. In the very rare circumstances that an own-label product slips through the net unexamined by the chairman, it is pulled off the shelves in all stores within hours.

Even once approved, products are regularly tested in extensive research and development (R&D) labs to ensure they meet high-quality standards. This applies particularly to own-label goods, which represent over 50 per cent of total sales, but only 25 per cent of stock lines.'R&D's main function is quality control of goods that bear our name,' explains Sir John. 'We'll only put our name on products as good as or better than the proprietary brand. The United States has had very little success with own-label because it only pushes price. We recognized when we started selling own-label products in the 1920s that every packet could affect our good name with the customer.' The labs make some 60,000 tests on food each year.

The fast growth of Sainsbury in recent years has been fuelled to a large extent by the need continually to improve the quality of service. 'We had to invest in new stores because the old ones were out of date,' he explains.

In the chapter on involvement, we examined how pride in ownership was in part a matter of respect for the product – if employees feel the product is inferior, it is hardly surprising that their general attitude towards the company as a whole is somewhat jaundiced. The importance of quality control as an employee *motivator* can be seen graphically in the events at British Leyland.

Michael Edwardes (the 'Sir' came later) concluded correctly that one of the factors contributing to low employee morale was the poor public regard for the product. It is very difficult to put one's heart and soul into the manufacture of something that has become a standing joke. Jaguar owners in the United States were supposed to have two vehicles: one for driving and the other to cannibalize for spare parts when the first broke down. So Edwardes made the launch of the first new car under the new management an exercise in employee morale building by hammering away to convince them its quality would be equal to or better than anything produced by competitors.

To an already tight and hectic engineering programme under pressure to get the production line operational, Edwardes added the extra pressure of frequent upgrading of specification. He talks of a 'commitment to perfection', which engendered a sense of excitement and caused previously demoralized employees to work exceptionally long hours. 'This new-found confidence was leading to the setting of tougher objectives for the car,' says Edwardes.

'The LC8 was more than just a car, it was the yardstick by which the whole company would be judged,' he comments in retrospect. Top management emphasized the commitment to beating the competition by driving Fiestas, Fiats and VW Polos to compare with the new car, then told the project team how much further it had to go to produce a better vehicle. The old spiral of defeat, demotivation, poor quality, and back to defeat had been broken at the point of quality. Once the internal concept of the product had moved from poor to high quality, it was relatively easy to impose a new cycle that moved through confidence in the product, to the reality of high quality, through success in the market and renewed confidence, back again to continuous quality improvement.

Hunger for market information

'Bejam has always been marketing oriented,' says Bill Perry, 'whilst in most retail companies it will not have figured until recent years. That is due to our relative youth and my background. Much of our energy has been devoted to researching customers' needs and behaviour. Good rapport with them is essential to the sort of specialized business that we operate. It is also vital that you do not waste space and distribution resource with the wrong lines particularly when you only have 4000 square feet of selling space. We have to test market thoroughly if we are not to play continuous musical chairs. Our store size, and the relatively limited range possible within it, is such that one can memorize sales line by line but it also imposes a greater need to make every inch work. Accurate marketing arithmetic leads directly to good quick decisions. I enjoy gambling but not at Bejam.'

Better known for the scale of its market research, however, is supermarket giant Sainsbury. Sir John has no doubt that keeping a close ear to the ground on changes of customer taste and needs is a major reason why his company has survived healthily into the 1980s while virtually every other big name in the grocery business before World War Two has disappeared or been taken over.

Sainsbury spends vast man-hours collecting and analysing any kind of market data that might give an edge to decision-making. Explained Sir John: 'We are unusual in the retail world in the importance we have always attached to [market research]. Data concerning the general marketplace in terms of the nation's economy, food trends and socio-economic environment are constantly updated and analysed. Trends are monitored and new sectors explored. Competitors' developments in terms of new stores, marketing strategies and prices are examined closely.'

A trade magazine carried this description of the Sainsbury process:

> An annual attitude survey, based on 2000 lengthy interviews in the home, helps establish where, how often and when people shop. Great weight is attached to what people think of Sainsbury's and the high street competition.
>
> By regularly taking the pulse of the high street, we understand better the shopping patterns by areas. We study what is being bought and where, how much is being spent and by whom, for every location in our trading area.
>
> Decisions of where we should try to open new branches are well grounded in market research. The profile of the potential customer, the volume of likely shoppers, the lines most likely to sell, the size of the car park, the extent of the competition and the potential turnover, are all closely examined.

One of the central functions of AGB is a research facility that monitors market developments around the world. It provides top management with regular reports, and also filters and redirects the information it gathers back around the world to the field units.

For our successful companies a close understanding of their markets is a prerequisite for an aggressive marketing thrust. Action is rooted in confidence that they know what they are doing and have the resources to accomplish their objectives, and this confidence is in turn rooted in the detailed information they gather about their customers and their competitors.

The volumes of market data are used as background for planning, both at corporate strategic and unit operational level. It might be assumed that they complicate the planning task, but in fact the opposite appears to be true. In most of our successful companies it is the comprehensiveness of the background data that allows the plan itself to be relatively brief and simple, because less allowance has to be made for the unknown.

The manufacturing companies in our sample also adopt a rigorous approach to analysing the market they operate in. This has two major benefits. It reduces the risk and hence the internal barriers to innovation; and it helps to focus attention back on fundamentals.

Market-oriented research and development

Racal's Harrison has a habit of asking young engineers the targeted costs of the piece of equipment they are developing. Anyone who doesn't know is in for a blistering. Says Harrison: 'If he doesn't know, he's not the man I need.'

Racal does not think twice about sending an engineer into untamed jungle to carry heavy equipment on his back for miles through swamps, rivers and tangled undergrowth along with military patrols. What better way to demonstrate to him just how important it is to the end-user to shave off those extra few pounds of weight from the equipment. 'We believe in encouraging engineers to test the equipment where it is to be used,' says Racal director of corporate relations Kenneth Ward.

Starting research and development with market need rather than technological possibility has been integral to the Racal philosophy from the company's early days. By the mid 1960s it had a strong reputation in UF radio equipment and an interest in moving into the supply of walkie-talkies to Third World armed forces.

All the equipment then available was designed to very high specifications, to work without fault at 120°F in the middle of the Sahara or at minus 60°F in the Arctic. Few developing nations needed or could afford that kind of specification. Racal developed a version in which all the trimmings were stripped away. The result? A tactical radio half the weight, one-third of the price and so simple that an operator could learn to use it in five minutes rather than several hours. Several years later Racal became the world leader in this defence equipment area. 'We simply went against the trend and gave people what they wanted,' says Ward.

Summary

Successful companies understand and interreact closely with their markets. This is not a surprising conclusion. Peters and Waterman certainly found the same thing for US companies and European research has demonstrated the same phenomenon.

One of the clearest expositions of this is found in the researches of Swiss professor Cuno Pümpin, of St Gallen Graduate School of Business Administration. Pümpin carried out a series of studies on thirty companies in German-speaking Europe, ranging in size from $26 million to $1.6 billion in annual sales. He subsequently validated his research by an examination of US and British companies, where he came up with similar results.

The technique Pümpin used was deceptively simple. He provided executives in each firm with a list of characteristics and asked them to identify which were both discussed most often and in greatest depth, and given funding most easily. From their answers he found that companies divided sharply into the introverted and the extroverted.

Top management in the introverted companies either tended to spend much of their effort, attention and resources in cost cutting and increasing margins, or to be heavily oriented towards engineering or technological goals. Some gave high attention to both. But in all cases, the introverted companies gave relatively little emphasis to customer or market issues, preferring to look for profit to matters over which they had more immediate control. The extroverted companies, on the other hand, placed greatest importance on marketing and sales, on customer satisfaction and service, on quality, or on a mixture of all three.

Pümpin's comparisons demonstrate clearly that extroverted companies generally perform much better in profit terms than introverted ones. This applied particularly to some severely depressed industries, where the few companies that shone with health usually turned out to be extroverted organizations, while their less successful cousins tended to be introverted companies.

He also found that the degree of agreement and common purpose across the company had a significant effect on profitability and growth. The clearer the corporate identity as either an introvert or an extrovert organization, the more successful it was. As a result, some basically extrovert companies did less well than they might have, because production management had not fully accepted the sales culture of the organization. By contrast, some introverted companies performed reasonably well, by virtue of focusing everyone's attention on the goal of cutting costs and increasing margins. In other words, what counts is unity of corporate doctrine.

Our postal survey of companies found few who felt their market orientation to be anything but excellent or well above average. While that is true in many cases, we might perhaps expect business and the economy to be in a rather healthier state if all those managing directors' and chairmen's opinions were accurate. Clearly the perception held by top management is not always reflected throughout the company culture.

Where a strong market orientation does permeate the whole organization, however, the benefits can clearly be seen. Everyone from shop-floor worker to finance director assumes that marketing is part of his job, not something to be relegated to a discrete functional department.

In a few of our successful companies the market orientation even penetrates to the shareholders. At a recent Bulmer's annual general meeting, for example, shareholders sparked off a lively discussion by demanding to know what they could do to help sell the company's products.

7 Zero basing

The young Charles Forte looked at three sites for his first milk bar and chose the most expensive, least renovated. 'Why that one?' asked the estate agent. 'I stood outside each for half a day with a stopwatch and counted the number of mouths walking past,' explained Forte.

One of the most frequent reasons given for the collapse of a large company is that it lost its way. Although top management thought they knew where they were going, they had strayed so far from the fundamentals of the business that they were swept out of their depth.

Our successful companies are almost fanatical about keeping contact with the fundamentals of their businesses. They have a clear picture of the business they are in and find security in remaining within that picture. Were a Racal unit to begin to move into a low-technology, mass-production consumer product it could expect to be pulled up sharply before it got very far. If a product that didn't meet the high value-for-money criteria imposed by Sainsbury somehow found its way on to the shelves, it would not be there for long – the most recent time such a thing happened, the product was cleared from all stores within three hours. Both companies constantly monitor and reassess what they are doing against a handful of fundamental principles which may not be written down yet are accepted across the organization as the right behaviour.

Most of those fundamental principles have been covered in the previous chapters. The zero-base perception is what ensures that they are followed. In some respects it is the opposite of the innovation perception, because it constantly pulls people back from flights of fancy or sudden tangential ventures. When Sir John Sainsbury refers to his company as 'traditionalists with a passion for innovation' he is describing the special tension that comes from pitting the zero-base and innovation factors against each other.

In the same way that these companies have to find an accommodation between the conflicting pull of autonomy and control, so too, they have to resolve the conflict between innovation and the need to hold to fundamentals. How they do so boils down to three common characteristics, namely:

- they stick to their last
- they pay great attention to detail, so they know when the fundamentals are slipping
- they keep their eye closely on the ball, evaluating what they are doing against the fundamentals

Sticking to the last

Appropriately enough, Clark's the shoemakers are passionate believers in the virtues of sticking to the last. 'Every time we've diversified it's been a disaster,' says one of the company's senior managers. 'We stay in shoes,' adds Daniel Clark firmly. To maintain the pace of its expansion, Clark's has had to develop vertically, acquiring retail outlets at one end and building up a substantial shoe machinery business at the other.

'Sticking to the things we do well is a strategic response,' claims Bejam's Perry. It, too, has found that diversions outside its basic areas of experience are ignominious failures. The process by which Plessey has reinvigorated its management and overall performance over the past fifteen years began with the divestment of all the odds and ends that simply didn't fit into the core of its business philosophy. 'We used to be in pumps, record turntables, steel, semiconductor packaging, wire, pastes and many other areas,' says Sir John Clark. 'From 1962 onwards we rationalized the areas we were in and got rid of everything that was not directly involved with defence electronics, professional and civil electronics, telecommunications, aerospace or solid state physics.'

United Biscuits chairman Sir Hector Laing has had to adapt his view of the business his company is in, as its growth outstripped the limitations of biscuit manufacture and obliged it to expand into other areas. 'I'm a huge believer in the shoemaker sticking to his last,' he says. 'I used to think I was in the biscuit business. Then in 1964, I thought I was in the long-life convenience foods business. By 1972 I had come to the conclusion we were in the stomach business.'

The belief that success comes from doing well what you know well runs unchallenged throughout our top companies. In part it is to do with maintaining a clear identity. The success of a brand image based on the company name depends on simple recognition of what the company is about. The association of Clark's with shoes, Sainsbury with food retailing and MFI with flat-pack furniture is almost unbreakable.

By contrast, it is noticeable that when the identity becomes confused, so do both customers and employees. One of the major problems behind Woolworth in its declining years was that fact that no one could be quite sure what it was selling. Similar confusion surrounded Boots the Chemist, where pharmaceuticals are now a minor part of a product range that spreads from tableware to hifi. Market research shows that for every £1 customers intended to spend in Boots, they actually spent only 74p – at least partly because they could not locate the items they wanted, even though they were somewhere there. Boots has since pushed up the percentage to nearer 90. Another example is the Tube Investments group, whose ill-considered attempt to impose a corporate identity on dozens of individually successful small subsidiaries served merely to convince everyone that the company didn't know what business it was in.

But what about the conglomerates? Aren't they exceptions to the rule? It seems basically not. All four conglomerates – Hanson Trust, BTR, Grand Metropolitan and Trafalgar House – have chosen to limit the bulk of their acquisitions and developments to groups of companies in very similar industrial circumstances. Hanson, for example, deliberately chooses mature, unexciting, low-technology industries such as bricks, garden tools or automotive equipment. Hanson describes himself as 'a carthorse, not a racehorse. If you want a racehorse you need someone like Clive Sinclair.' High-technology companies, he reasons, can all too easily become cash traps, and the time before they show a return on investment is usually much longer than in the maturer industries.

Trafalgar House's growth, too, has been to a consistent formula. Nigel Broackes explains: 'We choose only mature businesses. We are not in retailing because we don't know anything about it. With a slight exception in the case of Cunard, we have never gone into anything we felt we could not run better than the people there at the time.' The group takes great care to maintain an overall balance between asset-heavy and asset-light activities.

BTR's Sir Owen Green, in a rare exposition of his company's philosophy (see under Mills in Bibliography), explained how he and his colleagues determined the nature of their business in terms of 'not merely what we made and how we made it, but what needs were being served and what we were best equipped to do by attitudes as well as resources. We identified ourselves as being manufacturers of industrial components required in the fields of energy and engineering, materials handling and transportation, as well as in a number of special or niche activities of smaller volume potential but with relatively higher reward. We have not deviated in any significant way from that identity.'

Attention to detail

'We do the simple things well' is a Pritchard motto that finds expression in a raft of basic methods of tackling cleaning problems. Pritchard, for example, was the first cleaning company to develop estimating procedures that relied on accurate measurements of a building and how large an area staff could clean each hour, rather than a ballpark guess at the amount of cleaner time required. Old copies of the company's procedures manual can be found in the offices of many smaller cleaning firms, who use them as the basis for the calculation of their own contract tenders.

Lord Hanson recalls how his father's eye for detail took him to what seemed at the time to be ridiculous lengths. In the middle of the Canadian winter, the old man insisted that all the distribution company's trucks be cleaned, because it was bad for the company image. In vain did they explain that the trucks would swiftly become covered with a sheet of ice. The fundamental principle that good service and a clean appearance were inseparable could not be bent. The very fact that the old man went to such extremes rammed home the message.

Sir Ernest Harrison has a habit of ringing managers late at night to check a minor statistic in a speech he has to give the next day, because he is determined that what he says must be totally accurate. 'He is meticulous in his attention to detail,' says corporate relations director Ward. 'He makes sure what he says can't be disputed on fact and spends hours putting a speech right.'

Visitors to executives of Woolworth may be a little surprised to find themselves quizzed over the efficiency and courtesy of their reception at company headquarters. It is a sign that the new management has this same attention to detail. Anything that affects the public image of the company needs to be checked and monitored thoroughly.

The living doyen of attention to detail, however, has to be Sir John

Sainsbury. 'Retail is detail' has become a by-word for Sainsbury, and the principle is clearly put into effect with a thoroughness that still amazes long-serving and senior employees. The opening of a new store rarely passes without the chairman discovering something slightly wrong. 'He'll stand in the middle of an aisle and say: "There's something not right here,"' says director of branch operations Dennis Males. 'We just opened a store the other day. He walked in and saw iceberg lettuces at 58p and 74p. There were two sizes but because they were different varieties, they could weigh the same. He picked it up straight away. We should either have sold just the one variety, or put the information on the product. As it was, we were just confusing the customer and that's not acceptable.

'The managers expect it. They feel that no matter how well they do things, he can do them better.'

It can, of course, sometimes be frustrating for people down the line. 'Where big things are concerned, there's no problem in taking decisions,' says Males. 'But God help us on the little things!'

Keeping the eye on the ball

'Perry is a pain in the side to many of the managers here, but he certainly makes us re-examine everything we do,' says a Bejam manager. It is not a description with which Perry would quarrel. 'Having carefully framed something I will be its arch-critic,' he explains. 'If you have enough belief in yourself and your company you don't ever need to defend untenable positions. Too many things carry on too long in many companies because someone in a senior position has put his name to it, making it inviolable. Here there's no dread about parading your mistakes in front of others, junior or senior. Part of our recipe is constant watching and re-evaluation.'

Sacred cows are deliberately and routinely examined at Bejam to ensure they still fit current circumstances. A standard feature of Bejam shops, for example, used to be a monthly newspaper containing all the prices of products in the freezer centres. Routine questioning of whether the newspaper was still appropriate led to the realization that, in areas where there was heavy competition, it was slowing down the speed of the company's response. Competitors would obtain a copy the first day of issue and adjust their own prices immediately. The Bejam stores had to wait another month before they could make any additional changes. The newspaper was swiftly chopped, even though it had been a highly successful promotional tool to begin with, because it cut across a fundamental principle of Bejam's business – the need to respond to challenge swiftly and head on.

One benefit of zero basing is that companies recognize their mistakes sooner and are able to take quick and decisive action to correct them. When Clark's profits dipped in 1982, everyone accepted immediately that the company must have got away from one or more of the fundamentals. 'You have to control the entrepreneurial spirit because every time someone goes off to try something new, he loses sight of the core business,' says Daniel Clark. 'The lesson of the poor year in 1982 was that we had allowed too much experimentation.'

In seeking new markets, for example, the manufacturing side had lost its concentration on the style demands of the present customers, admits John Clothier. 'Come 1978, things were going very well indeed,' he recalls. 'We started to forget some of the key factors in our success formula. We didn't forget about quality or fit. But we did forget the style, and stopped innovating there.'

Getting back to basics meant going into the shops and watching what was happening there. Clothier and his colleagues saw the problem very quickly. 'I saw a lot of pitched battles between parents and children. The children were saying, "We don't like these shoes." The mother made them take the shoes the first time, but as the battle took place the next time, she thought again, "Why pay a high price for something my child doesn't want?"

'Once we realized what was wrong, we tackled the problem swiftly. This year, the only tears we saw at going back to school time were because we had run out of one of the preferred styles.'

'Our strength is not that we make impeccable decisions,' says Lord Rayner, the first non-family chief executive of Marks & Spencer, 'it is that we are self-critical. We recognize our mistakes and where improvements can be made.' Sieff, only half-jokingly, says that Rayner is lucky because he has been left so many mistakes he can get his teeth into.

The list of mistakes made and chopped quickly is quite lengthy across our sample companies – Asda with its Ukay Discount Centres, Bejam with its ill-fated foray into fast food, Trusthouse Forte into the travel business, which looked as if it had a great deal of synergy with hotels but eventually proved not to.

Associated Dairies' Noel Stockdale recalls one such saga in this way. 'If something isn't right, we pull out straight away. At one stage we had the bright idea of making biscuits in the stores. It made a lot of sense because we are the biggest retailer of biscuits. But in fact that was precisely the reason it didn't work.' The concept, they later realized, was ideal for a retailer who *didn't* have a major share of the biscuit market.

More important, however, is the fact that zero basing is so deeply ingrained into the culture of the top companies that they usually manage to avoid making such mistakes in the first place.

8 Innovation

'We are traditionalists with a passion for innovation' –
Sir John Sainsbury

Some organizations fear the future; others embrace it with enthusiasm. Although our sample of top companies clearly all have a distinct and stable culture to carry around with them, they also tend to enjoy experimentation within the areas they understand. They have a general openness to new ideas, although not always to ideas from outside; they value innovations that advance the corporate mission. They tend to see innovation not as another overhead that the company needs to stay in business, but as a flexible tool in the competitive game.

By and large these are not industries one would automatically turn to for models of innovation. Nor indeed do most of them sparkle with a constant display of new products. But they are frequently the first in the field with a radical new way of doing things. For example, Sainsbury's move into supermarkets was against all tradition and trends in Britain in 1950. The previous year Alan Sainsbury and fellow director Fred Salisbury had visited the United States to observe at first hand how supermarkets worked there. Experimental supermarket branches at Croydon, Eastbourne, Grange Hill and Debden led to the swift decision to convert all Sainsbury shops to the same model.

Clark's led the field in introducing the concept of autofill to its retail customers, and in doing so probably saved the independent high street shoe shop from extinction. Faced with the aggressive expansion of British Shoe Corporation to some 2000 shops, Clark's had to find some way to help the small retailers to compete. The solution it came up with went to the heart of the small retailer's problems – that he needed to maintain a relatively small stock, to maintain a high level of cash flow, but a large choice to satisfy customers' needs. These two contradictory demands were overcome by placing punched cards in each shoe box. At the end of each week, the retailer returns the cards and his stock is automatically replenished a few days later. New, more accurate methods of foot measurement in the pipeline will help to defend the company's service/quality image. Clark's is unusual in our sample of success in that its innovations tend to be defensive reactions rather than offensive pro-actions, but the reaction always switches on swiftly when needed.

Sir Lawrie Barratt uses innovation rather like a Viking used a battle-axe, laying about the competition to hack new growth opportunities out of a mature market. This rare zeal for constant innovation leads to an average of a major new product each year in an industry that last felt the draught of innovation with the invention of the damp course. Significantly, innovation for Barratt is a close-knit affair between product and marketing, with marketing constantly feeding production with new ideas as to what the home-buyer wants.

Trafalgar House, too, pushes its subsidiaries to innovate constantly. Cementation, for example, aims to produce at least one major new construction technique a year.

MFI is a company built on one major innovation, the concept of flat-pack furniture. The appeal of the concept is much more subtle than it appears at first sight. A great deal rests on the suppressed desire of most men to be seen as 'good with their hands'. Flat-pack furniture allows them to wrestle with building kitchen cabinets or fitted wardrobes with a reasonable certainty of getting it right and ending up with a professional-appearing job. Hunt compares it with the experience of Green's cake mix, which failed to sell well when all the housewife had to add was water, but took off dramatically as soon as the company changed the ingredients to require her to crack an egg into the mixture.

MFI has also innovated, however, in the design of its stores, pioneering the concept of a standardized design that consists of little more than a shell with maximum display space. Not only does this keep construction costs down, but it speeds up the building process by at least one-third.

Innovation is not, of course, simply a matter of new technology. It embraces all disciplines within a company, from marketing to finance, or distribution to training. Few of our companies felt that they were very successful at innovating across the board; rather, the main thrust of their innovation went into areas the company culture designated as critical. At STC, for example, Sir Kenneth Corfield says: 'We aim to be well up in innovation in social as well as technology matters.'

At Saatchi & Saatchi, the thrust of innovation is almost entirely into the advertising product. In an industry where creativity is a major part of the sales pitch, it could hardly be otherwise. The difference at Saatchi is the degree to which it will innovate. Designers and copywriters are constantly pushed to go beyond the limit and then be drawn back, rather than stop at what they think the customer will accept.

'We take a lot more risks on our advertisements than most of our competitors,' says Maurice Saatchi. 'And we keep urging our creative people to take more. We have had the same paragraph in our annual report for thirteen years. In my opinion Christopher Logue describes the process of creativity in the following way:'

> *Come to the edge.*
> *We might fall.*
> *Come to the edge.*
> *It's too high!*
> *COME TO THE EDGE!*
> *And they came*
> *and he pushed*
> *and they flew.**

In trying to isolate what our top companies did that enabled them to innovate where it matters, we came across five recurrent themes. These were by no means universal, but they do seem to represent a basic approach to the fostering of innovation. Those themes were:

- absence or removal of barriers to change
- natural curiosity about how things are done elsewhere
- international perspective
- directed research and development
- role of the chief executive

Absence or removal of barriers to change

Successful companies tend to create working environments where new ideas are welcomed, encouraged and, when accepted, implemented quickly. The elements of such an environment are not easy to define, but they certainly include:

- a clear framework of objectives within which innovation can be based
- constant information and feedback from management on where

* from *Ode to the Dodo/Poems 1953–1978* by Christopher Logue, Jonathan Cape Ltd.

ideas are most needed and what has happened to ideas already generated

- enough growth opportunity for people not to be overly concerned if change removes their current job, but to be enthusiastic about the opportunities in the next job within the firm
- organizational structures that facilitate the flow and implementation of new ideas
- high incentive and low punishment for taking acceptable and controlled risks

Clear framework of innovation objectives The clear strategic direction of our top companies makes it relatively easy for them to pinpoint the areas where innovation is most needed. While some innovation will just happen as a result of chance discovery, the vast majority of innovation has to be deliberately induced to order to be truly useful. Gordon Edge, chief executive of PA Technology, maintains that technological creativity, at least, 'flourishes under the constrained regime set by market and financial factors – so much so that the establishment of such constraints becomes the foundation stone of innovation rather than its boundary'. The more clearly the corporate objectives for innovation are drawn, the more practical and the more swiftly implemented the results are likely to be.

PA runs top-management study tours to Japan and issues a subsequent report based on the executives' observations. In 1983 the executives commented particularly upon the long-term vision of the Japanese companies in technical innovation. 'The determination to upgrade and improve already successful products was most impressive,' they reported, citing the example of Canon, whose research and development effort is organized on two levels. Each major product division, plus a central research and development facility, is looking five years ahead. An advanced-technology centre looks ten years ahead in close unison with the government's science and technology agencies and the universities.'

'Top management must be prepared to take a long-term view,' says David Sainsbury. 'If possible, it is obviously desirable to introduce change in an evolutionary way, but this cannot always be done. When six years ago we decided to go into hypermarket trading with British Home Stores, or more recently when we started up a chain of DIY centres with a Belgian partner, we could not do so gradually. In both cases we had to invest many millions of pounds and a great deal of management effort without knowing whether the formula we had devised was a profitable one. In the case of our hypermarket company, we now have a very profitable business, and in the case of our DIY business, the signs are good.'

Constant information and feedback from management Feeding this framework down the line helps to channel the thinking processes of people at all levels. Swift and certain responses to all ideas – even to say 'no', with an explanation why – help to maintain the impetus of innovation. Too many companies consciously or unconsciously indicate that they regard ideas from below as a nuisance. Ideas that do come up frequently get shunted aside to someone else's area of responsibility, going the rounds until they die in some corner of a filing cabinet. Then senior managers wonder why their own ideas fail to inspire the troops below. While it is not practical to expect the major innovations that change policy or strategy to emerge from below (though it can and does happen), top management often forgets that major innovations depend upon lots of smaller innovations to make them work, and that these smaller ones have to be generated down the line.

The Japanese, through their renowned quality circle and other schemes of employee involvement, have taken innovation from below to an art. At one extreme is Honda's remarkable bi-annual competition in which teams of employees from all over Japan are given the resources to design and build inventions. One aim is to encourage radical, new, patentable solutions to engineering problems. Another is simply to stimulate lateral thinking, while demonstrating to employees that innovation can be fun. At the other extreme is the equally remarkable success of the humdrum suggestion scheme, which even without quality circles has become an accepted part of working routine in Japanese industry.

With a few notable exceptions, British companies have manifestly failed to take advantage of the suggestion box. Yet those that have made a serious effort with the concept in recent years have generally been pleased with the results. Ian MacGregor, for example, instituted a special prize in British Steel for the best cost-saving idea each quarter. Individual winners receive a Mini-Metro; groups of people or quality circles receive steel-based goods of the same value. The average annual saving on each of these winning ideas is between £80,000 and £100,000.

West German industry, however, has gone even further. Backed by the country's Institute of Management, some one hundred and seventy firms have banded together to promote suggestion schemes. Volkswagen, for example, ensures that everyone who makes a suggestion receives a prize of some sort, and offers employees the chance to participate in a lottery that offers stereo sets, bicycles and holidays as typical prizes. The aim of the West German campaign is to raise the proportion of employees who take part in suggestion schemes from only 7 per cent to near the 28 per cent achieved by some computer companies. It is probably a fair assumption that most British companies are even further behind.

Security through growth opportunity The Japanese practice of job security (even though it only applies to a fraction of the work force and for a shorter working life than in Europe) does help to remove barriers to innovation, by negating the threat of redundancy. But successful British companies can often create a similar and possibly more healthy situation, simply by stressing growth. Such is certainly the case with Sainsbury, which has generated many thousands of jobs in recent years, and with AGB, where the whole company culture is based on growth through innovation. STC, although it has had to make drastic cuts in its work force to cope with the effects of new technology, now attempts to build in job guarantees to its strategic planning. Maintaining the current level of employment in 1984 means doubling sales by 1988. The objective, clearly articulated by top management and written into the detail of the long-range plan, is accepted as a reasonable if ambitious goal at all levels, because everyone has a stake in ensuring it happens.

Quite how companies can create and sustain this kind of motivation when there is little or no growth or when growth is insufficient to counter-effect job losses from new technology is another issue. It seems that while success often depends on innovation, innovation also to a large extent depends upon success.

Organizational structure How to organize for innovation has been the subject of reams of academic study and hundreds of learned articles in journals such as *Harvard Business Review, International Management* and *Management Today*. The answer seems to be that there is no one right way, but that the structure of the company has a significant impact.

Although the high-technology companies in our sample are all highly decentralized in operational terms, they all maintain some central control on research and development. Racal, for example, effectively splits the research and the development into two separate functions. Most of the development work is done in the operating units, where it can be closely related to their individual marketing programmes. This avoids the problems of competition for scarce time and resources by the units of a central organization, when swift action may be essential to beat the competition to the market. The subsidiary manager decides how much of his resources will go into development work and is able to make or approve changes to the projects quickly whenever a new need or a new technology arises.

At the same time, Racal maintains three main laboratories for advanced research. This is inappropriate in the operating units, says Harrison, 'because it never actually happens there. They are too concerned with getting stuff out of the doors to the customer.' The operating units buy time at the central laboratories out of their own budgets, with several units often sharing the costs of supporting a large research programme. They can second their own engineers to the centre to work alongside the research team and bring back the know-how. The research may result in a completely new product, for which a new company is spun off; Comsec, Racal's communications security company, arose in this way, for example. Similarly, new variations on existing products may be moved into a company formed for the purpose. When Racal Acoustics developed its military helmets to meet a need in coal mining, so many other potential non-military applications emerged that a new company was formed to exploit them.

The final element to the organization of Racal's research and development is what Harrison calls a 'free spend' – forward-looking research carried out at the margins of the operating companies' budgets, but not covered by Racal's central research and development facilities. 'They can do anything they like with this money,' he says. 'They can even duplicate research elsewhere if they want to. The only stipulation is that they must make the results available to the rest of the group.'

Overlaying all this is the assumption throughout that development costs will be met by Racal, either as a group or as an operating unit. Harrison believes that this self-sufficiency – 95 per cent of all Racal's research and development is self-funded – is critical to achieving market-oriented research and to containing research and development costs. The effectiveness of the approach is demonstrated, for example, by Racal's behaviour when it lost a tender, on price, for a major development in frequency-hopping radio for the United States armed forces.

Racal decided to go ahead anyway, developing and marketing its own system more than two years before the US equipment was ready.

Plessey adopts almost the opposite approach with regard to funding, relying heavily on government development contracts. It is not a situation Sir John Clark particularly likes. 'Up until recently the funds spent by the public sector in private industry were directed exclusively at products for the public sector itself. The exportability of the products was zero. We have been waging a war to get this changed, and in the telecommunications sector we now have an internationally acceptable, comprehensive range of product.'

STC's product innovation profile is closer to Racal's. It has both central and unit-based research facilities, for example. It is also adept at combining 'technology push' with 'market pull', seizing opportunities to create markets from chance discoveries in the laboratories rather than simply identifying market needs and attempting to meet them first.

'We have institutionalized entrepreneurship,' claims Corfield. 'For many years now we have had a new-business board, which is well publicized within the company. People come before the board to make proposals for new ventures. The board has funds to give them, if they make their case. It can be quite rough with them if the idea is insufficiently thought through. Several of our major products, such as the radio pager, have been derived from this route.'

The new-products board was originally based on a standard ITT pattern. Under independent ownership it has been devolved almost entirely to the operating divisions, who have their own budgets for new ventures, with only very expensive but viable project ideas being pushed up to group level. 'We at headquarters are setting up instead an entrepreneurial bank,' says Corfield. 'We are working on a scheme that would provide proposers of new ventures with equity in the idea. After two or three years we will have some decisions to make. Either the venture will have gone on well and be vulnerable to takeover or it will have been unsuccessful. If it is successful, STC would be likely to retain the right to buy out the management. If the entrepreneur feels the business is better than the company sees it, he would have the opportunity of a management buy-out.'

Corfield does not see this scheme as a major source of growth for STC, expecting most growth to come from traditional internal development. But as a means of training managers in entrepreneurial thinking and keeping them alert to the market possibilities of the technology under their control, it has much to recommend it. It also creates a suitable environment for the organizational mavericks who are so important in keeping change processes going. 'A lot of companies say they want innovation, but they don't really want innovators,' he points out.

A strong perception that innovation has to be managed also characterizes many of the medium- and low-technology firms. At AGB, for example, where organizational mavericks make up a high proportion of middle and senior management, the group maintains control over major innovation projects through a committee representing all the key interests in the company, including computer software and finance. Mike Head, the secretary of the committee, acts as a progress chaser on the thirty to forty projects on the cards at any one time. 'Research and development is an incubating process,' says Audley, explaining that the committee both reviews ideas for viability and agrees development investment.

Allied Breweries' Strachan sees constant innovation as one of the central pillars of his strategic growth programme. Over a period of years he has taken the company's technical centre at Burton on Trent from a policing and monitoring unit, specializing in quality control, to a more broadly based, forward-looking organization aimed at helping the operating units to innovate. By raising the calibre of research staff and putting pressure on the operating units to originate their own new projects, he has persuaded the researchers to activate ideas they have had for years, but never been encouraged to present for consideration. At the same time, he has attracted and retained bright young marketing men to work alongside the scientists, with the prospects of changing methods of brewing and handling beer and the development of new drink products.

Strachan has also used the decentralized nature of the brewing company to encourage innovation. Instead of taking ideas from the units and developing them centrally, the development responsibility gets pushed right back again, to the originating unit. 'We are trying to create the "invented here" syndrome,' he explains. 'For example, we will hit the market in 1984 with new packaging for take-home beer. We gave the job of developing the packaging to the unit that thought of it, telling them: "You do all the work and you'll take all the credit." They did it because they had a clear motivation.'

None of these companies minimizes the difficulties of stimulating innovation, however. M&S's Sieff candidly admits: 'We have still not found a way to deal with constructive mavericks.' People who want to make swift or radical change find it tough going within a centralized bureaucracy. Sieff recalls the case of Peter Wolff, who ruffled so many feathers that when he asked permission to attend a course in the United States, he was told by the personnel department he could have a one-way ticket. Wolff is now chief executive of a major M&S supplier, S.R. Gent.

High incentive and low punishment for taking acceptable and controlled risks To a large extent this has already been covered in previous chapters, but it is clear that innovation and risk are very closely associated in the minds of top management of our successful companies. Says David Sainsbury: 'By definition, innovation requires initiative, doing things in unconventional ways, and risk-taking, and people will not enthusiastically introduce change if they feel that the safest way to get to the top of their organization is to stay out of trouble.'

At GEC Lord Weinstock tries to instil the attitude that the risks associated with research and development innovation are an essential part of staying in business. 'I don't regard R&D as risk-taking,' he says, 'because there is no way a company like this can exist without R&D.'

Natural curiosity about how things are done elsewhere

Several years ago a dozen Pritchard managers, including the chief executive, went out to Australia to clean floors for a month, because they wanted to learn how it was that the Australian employees cleaned faster than those in England. The lessons they learned gave the company an extra edge in new tenders.

This close interest in how things are done elsewhere, and willingness to learn from anyone, is a feature of several of our top companies. 'We have no shame in copying a good idea,' says R.H. Sellier of Trafalgar House subsidiary Cementation. Both marketing and research and development are outward looking, seeking bright ideas wherever they originate.

There are, however, examples of just the opposite. Maurice Saatchi admits disarmingly: 'We have a rather arrogant attitude that says, "What is there that we could learn from others when we are the best in the business?"'

International perspective

Closely intertwined with natural curiosity is the awareness among the top companies that the UK is simply too small to be a viable market on its own and that true excellence only comes from competing on the world stage. This is not particularly true of the retailing firms – indeed it is hard to think of *any* retailers that have been really successful internationally, perhaps because of the degree of adaptation required to each national culture. But the top company retailers do keep a very close eye on developments in other countries, especially the United States. Sainsbury's acquisition of a New England retailing chain was at least partially motivated by the desire to gain early experience in new retail techniques before transplanting them to the UK.

'A good intelligence system', says David Sainsbury, 'alerts management to technological and competitive changes. We have built up over a number of years a network of contacts throughout the world, which keeps us in touch with most of the innovations that take place in retailing. A large number of our directors visit the US or Europe each year to see what developments are occurring, and this leads to a mass of innovations in the way we run our business.'

Plessey, after years of cossetting from the British telecommunications authorities, does not have an international perspective to be proud of. Sir John Clark candidly admits: 'Our market shares [of international business] are so pathetic we could expand in any direction we wished.' Gaining that international exposure is a central plank in the company's development strategy.

The majority of our top companies, however, have a strong and consistent presence overseas and a regular flow of ideas and experimentation between the overseas and the domestic operations. Barratt, for example, is expanding more rapidly in California than in the UK. One advantage of this move is that the company should be better able to weather cyclical downturns in the British housebuilding market when it reaches saturation coverage of the UK.

'We only have fifty-six million people here in Britain and a lot of our products can't be exported because their shelf life isn't long enough,' says Sir Hector Laing. United Biscuits is number two in its market in the United States and uses its company there to forewarn it of moves by the giant US-based international food companies. The US subsidiary also provides a useful trial ground for defensive strategies against those companies. In addition, United Biscuits has a presence in Japan, not least, says Sir Hector, in order to gain an insight into new engineering and production methods. 'All our companies keep looking round the world for products they can do something with,' says UB director Bill Gunn.

Several of our more recently established top companies, such as Racal and Saatchi, have had international aspirations in their objectives from the beginning. Saatchi's aim to become the biggest advertising agency in the world goes back to its earliest days and automatically caused its managers to assume an international perspective. It has also built up much of its business strategy on the theme that client companies with international sales need clearly identified international brands and that only a truly internationally oriented advertising agency can provide the kind of comprehensive service international brands need.

The nature of the international exposure of these companies is active rather than reactive. Overseas subsidiaries have very high autonomy and are expected to sort out their own problems. But they also typically receive a great deal of top-management time and attention, assuring them that they are not 'forgotten outposts'. 'My headquarters doesn't understand me!' is less often heard in these companies than in multinationals in general.

BOC, for example, has become so internationally oriented that the majority of its activities are now outside the UK, with the home country accounting for only one-third of group profits. Its group chief executive, Dick Giordano, is an American who spends at least half of his time in the overseas subsidiaries, particularly in the United States. Giordano was the chief executive of Airco before it was acquired by BOC and was swiftly promoted to his current position by a perceptive Sir Leslie Smith. The company superimposes on the autonomy of the overseas subsidiaries a clear divisional structure on product lines to co-ordinate global strategy, particularly in product development.

Lord Hanson also spends a major proportion of his time in the company's US operations, from a 'second head office' in California. He has four homes, two each in the United States and Britain, and commutes between them as the need arises around the Hanson empire. You can't run a substantial business in the United States on fleeting week-long trips, he explains. To really understand the US market and way of doing business you have to live there at least part of the time.

This need for international input into the company's thinking processes is behind the growth in the United States of international advisory councils, made up of leading businessmen from other countries. These worthies meet several times a year with the executive board, keeping the company up to date with international developments and evaluating corporate strategy against their intimate knowledge of their own countries.

A brief examination of some of the more successful financial institutions suggests that an international mentality is of value there, too. Fast-growing Britannia Arrow, for example, has targeted the United States and the Far East as priority areas for expansion. Selected board members of the overseas companies Britannia Arrow has acquired are given posts on the operational committees of the British company to ensure a constant cross-fertilization of culture and ideas.

What all these companies are demonstrating is a genuine commitment to global strategic thinking, to using the resources available to them around the globe – or at least in the key chosen areas – in a synergistic way. Significantly, this has been identified as one of the key reasons for the success of Japanese multinationals. Dr Lawrence G. Franko, professor of International Business Relations at the Fletcher School of Law and Diplomacy in the United States, argues that while it is rare to find a Western multinational that thinks in truly global terms, it is rare to find a Japanese multinational that does not.

Firms in the US have tended to be backward in the design of international strategy both because of an innate parochialness and because the domestic market is so large. Britain's circumstances and need for global strategies are much closer to those of the Japanese – our market is too small for the kind of long-term growth associated with successful companies, and exports have to provide a large part of our gross national product for economic survival.

So an international perspective should be axiomatic for successful British companies. One of the factors that may explain why it is not is that the domestic market lacks the fierce, not to say ruthless, competition that characterizes most consumer and capital-goods markets in Japan. Japanese companies fight each other over price and quality before they tackle the rest of the world. Products that survive in that environment will usually have an edge over competition anywhere else. It is to achieve that edge at home that much of Japanese corporate strategy is aimed, through, for example, efficient use of cheap labour in Third World countries. It comes as second nature for successful Japanese companies to apply global strategy to their assaults on European and North American markets. That the Japanese multinationals are held up as models for companies in other countries to copy is scarcely surprising, for what we see are the survivors of a jungle where only the very fittest fight their way into international competition. Sharper domestic competition among British firms could well help to catapult increasing numbers into the ranks of international excellence.

Directed research and development

Research and development in the top companies tends to revolve around defined market needs and to be closely targeted in matters such as end price. Research and development spending appears to be relatively high compared to the rest of the market sector, but this is difficult to define because of differences between companies in assessing what constitutes research and development. Where technology push is important, in the high-technology companies, it is still subservient to strict market analysis and a tacit understanding that development cash goes where the highest market return can be expected.

The mature industries' approach is summarized well by BTR's Sir Owen Green, who writes: 'Our technologies have developed from basic-materials sources such as steel, rubber and the tonnage plastics, almost entirely from observation of customer needs. An early recognition of the advantages, for example, of glass reinforcement of polymers in stiffness/lightness/corrosion resistance and "shapability" has given us a lead in this field in the UK .... The development of high-performance plastics for arduous duties – acid protection, extreme heat environment, buoyancy and the like – has allowed us to present more effective materials and products to the customer .... Pure research is not for us; development and application are our forte.'

Significantly, the PA study tour's report on Japanese innovation also refers strongly to 'close links to the marketplace. Canon lays great stress on the importance of the interface between research and development and the market. Personnel are sent overseas for at least two years to obtain a thorough insight into local market needs, which in turn provides a major input into their strategic R&D efforts.'

Role of the chief executive

We saw when we looked at the successful companies' approach to leadership that top management's attitude and behaviour has a strong influence on behaviour throughout the company, and this is particularly true as regards innovation. If the chief executive makes it clear that he is genuinely interested in innovation and that people who innovate are valued and rewarded, then in a well-motivated organization people will respond.

Dr Maurice Sage, director of market analysis company BPA, and a former executive with both Philips and EMI, has spent several years studying the role of innovation in successful and unsuccessful firms. His conclusion is that companies which innovate well have chief executives who are directly involved in the innovation process. 'Top management in many companies doesn't get involved enough in product development,' he says. The problem turns out to be particularly acute in decentralized companies, where delegation by top management of responsibility for innovation all too often means that it simply doesn't happen, he claims, adding that even in centralized companies, 'if top management leaves new products to R&D or marketing departments, then they are ducking their responsibilities'.

Sage's views were strongly backed up by the *Financial Times*, which pulled together the opinions of a variety of experts on both sides of the Atlantic. Christopher Lorenz summarized the experts' opinions in this way:

> Top managers with little technical experience, and who have been educated to focus their attention on short-term issues, see technology as complex, long-term, narrow (just research and development) and highly uncertain. They are not only 'technology-averse' ... but they often find it downright intimidating.
>
> Whether or not they also make the mistake of underspending on technology, they therefore delegate the management of it, either well down the line, or to a senior executive. To do the latter might be all well and good, except that they don't then pay much attention to what he tells them.

The *Financial Times* article also quotes Dr William Summers of Booz Allen as saying: 'Many chief executives have surrendered control over this critical aspect of their business. While management tends publicly to espouse the importance of technology, few companies approach it as a strategic issue.'

One of the almost inevitable results of lack of top-management involvement in innovation, especially in technology, is that R&D and marketing set themselves different goals. Whichever is responsible for new products becomes more timid in the ventures it is prepared to undertake because it cannot count on whole-hearted support from other departments. In successful companies, observed Sage, the interplay between marketing and research and development was highly developed and there was close agreement on objectives. This situation did not occur of its own accord; it was a natural result of close top-management interest and involvement in setting strategic goals for innovation, and monitoring their progress.

STC's Corfield is a good example of how this kind of top-management pressure can work. He has a whole string of patents in his own name and takes a deep personal interest in the technical problems his engineers are attempting to solve. The typical chief executive site visit is rather like a royal tour – full of politely feigned interest and a lot of handshaking. Corfield, however, cannot resist getting involved in scientific puzzles, even if it wrecks a carefully organized set of management meetings later in the day.

'On one such occasion,' recalls his PA, Duncan Lewis, 'he ambled into the laboratories and got talking to a team who had been working on a difficult project for three years. He took one look and made some suggestions. He and the scientist in charge sparked each other off and eventually they resolved the problem on the spot. That got around the company quickly.'

Allied Breweries' Strachan is not a technologist, nor are the innovations he is looking for necessarily technology-based, but he, too, believes that top management has to lead innovation. 'You have to have a commitment to innovation,' he says. 'How else can you have a genuine competitive advantage? By encouraging people to be innovative, you show that you are committed to backing them.'

David Sainsbury, too, is a passionate believer that innovation can only become endemic with top management backing and example. He declares: 'Top management must ... be convinced that innovation is essential to the survival and prosperity of the business, and they must also make certain that everyone in the organization is aware of that conviction.'

Summary

Innovation in our successful companies is on the whole offensive, not defensive. Where it is defensive, it tends to be either in the form of strategic positioning to protect an existing market lead or as a swift counter-attack. In the latter, some of our top companies have had something to teach the US companies they have acquired. Sir Hector Laing recalls that when United Biscuits bought US biscuit manufacturer Keebler in 1974, 'they wouldn't move anything unless Nabisco did it first'. Now the US company has the same attitude as the rest of the group. 'When Proctor and Gamble suddenly threw a new product into a long-established market, they were ready to take it on head-on. Their attitude was "all of a sudden, this has become interesting".'

9 Integrity

'I attach more importance to integrity than to ability' –
Sir John Clark

One of the surprises in our interviews at chief executive level and below was the passion with which our successful companies embraced integrity as an essential part of their culture. This clearly was not window-dressing. Each company was convinced that without absolute integrity the business simply could not operate.

The reaction of these companies to any aspersions on their integrity is swift and vehement. Normally staid and placid chairmen's blood will boil at the suggestion that their company has been dishonest, sharp-practising or deliberately negligent. When a zealous local health inspector booked a Trusthouse Forte hotel on a string of items relating to the hygiene of its kitchens, Lord Forte took it as a personal insult. There was never any suggestion of simply pleading guilty and avoiding publicity. THF fought the case tooth and nail, winning all but seven of the points and taking the rest to appeal. It even took advertising space in national newspapers to state its case.

Sir Lawrie Barratt's reaction to criticism of the timber-framed houses which make up a large part of his production was similar: 'We have to protect the integrity of the group name at all costs.' The *World in Action* programme that cast doubts on the durability of the homes shook confidence in the firm both in the City and among potential customers.

Sir Lawrie went straight into the attack, putting the company's case forcefully and launching overnight a twenty-year guarantee to 'express the supreme confidence we have in our products'. Subsequent reports by the Building Research Establishment and the National House Building Council gave the timber-framed homes a clean bill of health.

Much the same reaction occurred when the company was criticized over the resale value of the houses it sold complete with fittings. Barratt's response was an immediate commitment to buy back at the original price any houses whose owners could not resell them during the first two years of occupation. A second *World in Action* programme on this theme elicited an aggressive advertising campaign putting the company's point of view.

The perception of integrity runs much deeper than this, however. It extends to all areas of these companies' activities, both internally and externally. It is not simply an absence of wrongdoing, but a positive attitude towards 'doing the right thing', which applies equally to customers, employees, suppliers and to the public at large.

Integrity towards customers

Implicit within the marketing approach of all the successful companies is the concept that trust is the cement of the relationship with their customers. The thought that a customer would feel he could not trust them would give most of these chairmen apoplexy.

This feeling is particularly strong among the retailers, whose customer front line is much more visible than in the manufacturing or service companies. For example, the main reason why Sainsbury fought long and hard against trading stamps in the 1960s was not simply that they eroded trading margins, but that they did not give the customer the best deal.

Lord Sainsbury refused steadfastly to countenance having trading stamps in his stores 'because we believe that the Sainsbury image and brand of marketing are based on good value and quality and not on gimmicks and sales promotion techniques, which raise the cost of distribution'. The idea of preying on people's weakness for wanting something for nothing offended the corporate morality.

When the trading-stamp war was at its hottest, Lord Sainsbury was quoted as saying: 'Our image is of quality, value, cleanliness, not coupons, stamps, music, prices you can't assess because everything is twopence off, windows plastered with posters so you can't see in. Our shops are clean, tidy, hygienic to look at – not gimmicky fun fairs.' In the end, the consuming public decided it agreed with him and trading stamps went the way of all passing fads.

Insistence on dealing fairly and openly with the customer was behind the packaging philosophy of Bejam. 'I'm considered a fetishist about honesty,' says Perry. Then he admits disarmingly: 'I learnt it from Sainsbury and Marks & Spencer. When we started, the best two examples to learn from were those companies, and nothing has changed. Honesty is there in those two organizations through the tiles.'

One way Bejam put that lesson into effect was to ensure that all its own-label goods had see-through wrappers. 'Most other manufacturers are forever putting products in boxes, with flattering pictures on the outside. So there is a dramatic level of disappointment when customers open up the boxes. For example, they will show brilliant-white fish fingers, or meat pies packed with meat, when the reality is very different. We show the customer the uncooked pastry.

'It pays off commercially. Our sales of sausage rolls in see-through bags dwarf those sold in boxes, because the housewife can see the size and shape.'

Integrity towards employees

When Sir Ernest Harrison travels around the Racal empire, he frequently talks about the need for the company to return the loyalty that employees show to their operation.

That same paternalistic concept of loyalty to hard-working employees is reflected in many other successful companies. Although a few of our companies still have something of a hire-and-fire reputation, most will simply put people who do not make the grade into jobs where they do not have a critical impact on group or unit profitability. Trusthouse Forte, for example, tends to move unsatisfactory hotel managers around until they either find a niche where they can perform, or are relegated to a staff position where they can do little harm. Clark's of Street, too, has a reputation for doing the same.

Unless managers commit gross misdemeanours, their jobs are highly secure in many of these companies. Sir Lawrie Barratt, for example, claims: 'Anyone who joins Barratt has a job for life. If he doesn't, it's our fault.'

Of course, this approach is a two-edged sword. It would be very easy to create immobile layers of sub-standard middle management, blocking promotion routes and stultifying innovation and growth. The reason this does not appear to happen is that the companies apply two standards, one for the critical tasks, where dynamism and entrepreneurial flair are prerequisites, and one for the peripheral tasks, which are necessary but make little direct contribution to cash flow or profitability, yet where loyalty is still a productive element.

For the critical tasks, low performance is not tolerated. Managers who fail to perform know they will be transferred. For the less critical tasks (training, for example, falls into this category in many of the companies of our sample and so, frequently, does computing) top management is prepared almost to turn a blind eye. The cost of some inefficiency in areas that are not perceived to matter is weighed against the benefits of being able to move low performers out of key jobs without drama. Knowing that they can retain a lower-pressure, lower-reward job with the company also encourages low-performing employees to accept what happens more easily than if the only alternative were out.

In parallel with this ambivalent attitude goes an acceptance that to be fair to employees, it is essential to let them know exactly where they stand. 'You have to tell people if they are doing a lousy job,' says Bejam's personnel manager Mike Jones.

This is a two-way street, insists a GrandMet senior manager: 'The truth is an important feature that must run through the whole company. Tell it as it is; don't tell me what you think I want to hear. Don't tell your bosses that things are OK when they're not. Be honest in communication.'

One of the few firing offences in GEC, says Lord Weinstock, is for a manager 'not to be frank'.

Sieff, too, tries hard to ensure that 'when a job is well done people receive credit visibly and vocally. It means that when a job is done badly, they accept criticism.'

The *perception* by the employees that the company will treat them fairly is as important, if not more so, than top management's belief that fair dealing is integral to the company's way of working. Only by very close personal monitoring can the chief executive be sure that the standards of fairness he expects to see are in fact applied, and that people all the way down the line share his vision.

The acceptance that the company really is fair and trustworthy has several times enabled United Biscuits, for example, to weather storms that could otherwise have shipwrecked all the careful years of investment in employee communications and welfare. When it announced the imminent closure of its Liverpool factory, United Biscuits put at risk its reputation as a socially concerned employer. Unemployment in the area was so high that few of the laid-off employees could expect to find alternative jobs. But the company's willingness to consider solutions put forward by the employee representatives, and to pay for expert advice from outside consultants to devise possible alternative plans, meant that even when the closure decision was ratified, most people accepted the logic and inevitability of the company's decision. Unpalatable as the closure was, it was difficult to see how it could have been approached with greater fairness.

Integrity towards suppliers

The company history of Marks & Spencer, published in 1969, describes how the philosophy developed 'that the manufacturer, the retailer and the consumer were parts of a single and continuous economic process in which each had a common interest'. All of the retail companies and many of the manufacturing companies have a reputation for driving hard bargains with their suppliers, to maintain low prices and high margins in the shops. Yet they also have the reputation of being fair and of seeking long-term relationships with suppliers.

Because top management looks constantly to the long-term growth and survival of the company, it makes sense to forge links with suppliers who can support long-term as well as short-term objectives. M&S, for example, has some suppliers who date back to the earliest days of the company, 100 years ago. No M&S supplier makes a quick and easy fortune out of the high street chain; but the supplier's margins are enough to assure the continued capital investment needed to upgrade quality and productivity regularly. 'We are only as good as our suppliers,' is a saying the Sieffs are particularly fond of.

'Suppliers don't resent toughness, as long as they can trust what you say,' says Bejam's Perry. 'As buyers we are more attractive than most other companies because we try to take the supplier's needs into account, too.' Courtesy and consideration for the supplier include making sure that bad news does not come as a surprise. There is no question of playing suppliers off against each other to bid down, and when a current supplier seems unlikely to meet a projected target for the future price he is told well ahead of time, to allow him either to improve his production and reduce unit costs, or to seek alternative outlets.

Said *Management Today* in a profile of Bejam in 1982: '"Bejam is loyal to suppliers," says one Findus executive, "and sometimes loyalty isn't a prime consideration."'

The sense of common interest between supplier and retailer also finds expression in new-product development. Still following in the footsteps

127

of M&S and Sainsbury, Bejam regularly develops new products in collaboration with long-standing suppliers. For example, it created with Bowyers a complete range of bakery products, which the customer simply has to thaw and bake. The regional test marketing of the products was so successful that the national launch had to be abandoned because all the production capacity was already being used. In general, Bejam allows the suppliers to supply the rest of the trade with new products under a different brand name, once its own stores are fully supplied. The reasoning is that, in a market where someone else is sure to copy the idea to supply other retailers, better the advantage should go to a Bejam supplier than to anyone else.

Non-retailers take a similar pragmatic attitude to relationships with suppliers. Sir Lawrie Barratt puts a great deal of marketing effort into ensuring that, in spite of ups and downs in the general house markets, his operating companies maintain a steady cycle of building. One reason for maintaining that cycle is to hold the confidence of suppliers. 'How can we expect them to gear up to a high rate of production if they are not confident we won't be closing down sites suddenly?' he asks.

'United Biscuits', says Sir Hector Laing, 'doesn't chop and change suppliers just for a pound or two here and there.' With its eye on the long term it is often prepared to pay over the odds in the short term. For example, it supported the independent millers, even though they were more expensive, because it saw the long-term disadvantage of reducing competition to a very small number of very large suppliers.

Clark's, whose golden rule for dealing with suppliers is 'Seek out the best and stick with them', has even applied the M&S supplier/retailer approach in reverse. Its own experience in shoe retailing has given it the expertise to run its own consultancy, which specializes in advising smaller retailers how best to display goods, fit out shops and train staff.

Clark's also goes to great pains to be scrupulously fair in its trading relations with suppliers. 'We pay their bills promptly, for a start,' says Cotton. 'We tell them when the leather is a little under the estimated amount and they should credit us; but also when it's a little over and they should debit us.'

Integrity towards the public at large

Ian MacGregor makes the point strongly that many companies have been seduced into accepting a concept of social responsibility that distracts them from the first priority of any business – creating wealth. It is diffi-cult to accuse any of our most successful companies of being distracted in this way, although it is noticeable that some of the British companies that make most noise about social responsibility are absent from our sample.

Where integrity comes into play most effectively in dealings with the external world is in responsiveness to significant moral issues. Success-ful companies will not risk the good currency of their corporate brand name by ignoring strong public moral feeling. By the same token, they appreciate the value to the maintenance of the brand name of being associated with responsible and caring behaviour. Social responsi-bility, then, is an essential part of the marketing profile.

Marks & Spencer, Sainsbury and United Biscuits are typical of the inner core of successful companies who see the benefits of a pro-active stance on social issues. They attack these issues with the same intensity and planning that they put into any other significant management task. Most important, they can afford to put something back into society because they are immensely profitable.

When Clark's had an official strike in 1984, it mortified top manage-ment, even though the stoppage was very brief. The company self-image of fairness in all circumstances simply never envisaged such a possi-bility. The event was probably more traumatic to both sides of the dispute than a loss on the group profit and loss account might have been.

It is significant that the only time anyone can remember Daniel Clark giving a direct order was when the integrity of the company was at stake. The issue was whether the company would renounce the use of leather cured with sperm whale oil. The initial reaction from the company, when it was asked by conservationist groups for such an undertaking, was that it had no control over its suppliers. The pressure from the conservationists grew and there was even talk of organizing a boycott of Clark's shoes.

At this point Daniel Clark stepped in and issued an edict. Not only would the company adopt an immediate policy of buying only leather cured without sperm whale oil, but it would invest in expensive spec-troscopic analysis and testing equipment to check that supplies con-formed to the new specifications. A few suppliers demurred, but Clark's is such a major customer that most readily agreed. Six months later Clark's was able to report that at least 98 per cent of its supplies were free of sperm whale oil. Typical of its Quaker background, the company would not claim 100 per cent, on the ground that it had not checked every single bale of leather to come into its warehouse.

Summary

'We have one core value,' says STC's Sir Kenneth Corfield, 'mutual respect between all the people inside the company and between people inside and outside it.'

The integrity factor guides the thinking throughout the organization, establishing high moral norms that provide automatic responses to ethical problems, and making top-management intervention (as in the Clark's sperm whale oil incident) rare.

The reverse side of the coin is that all of these audiences – especially employees and suppliers – tend to return the compliment, treating the company with the integrity it demands of them. Essential to that reflected integrity is an understanding by managers that they must do all they can to stick to their promises on profit and performance. 'No professional manager can hold up his head if he keeps breaking promises,' says Plessey's Parry Rogers.

'*Up the Organization* had a valid point when it advised "If all else fails, try honesty",' says Bejam's Perry. 'But it's even more profitable to start with honesty in the first place.'

10   The family/founder influence

Leadership style as part of company culture is heavily influenced in many of our successful companies by the character and reputation of the founder or recent family chairmen. In all cases there are anecdotes – some amusing, some alarming – that are instantly recognizable as belonging only to these people.

John James Sainsbury, the great-grandfather of the company's current chairman, was a man with a passion for orderliness, detail and self-help. He was the product of a generation that added humane values to the Victorian work ethic, while still espousing the virtues of hard work, thrift and self-discipline. Brought up close to one of London's major street markets, at the New Cut in Lambeth, John Sainsbury learnt early that for most of the people of London, buying food was at best an adventure, at worst a risk of contagion.

When he set up as a dairyman in 1869, Sainsbury was following in the footsteps of his father-in-law. But he brought to the business his own fiercely held ideas of how a food retailer should operate. 'My great-grandfather believed that high quality could go with low prices and however impoverished the housewife was she must still have the choice of buying the best quality available,' writes Sir John. 'Secondly, he believed that cleanliness and freshness were what people wanted if only they had the opportunity of getting them.'

This preoccupation with low prices and wholesomeness has stayed with the company to this day. The current chairman and his executive colleagues still personally taste every new product before it is allowed on the shelves. Sainsbury's margins are constantly under review and are highly competitive.

Sainsbury established what was in the late 1800s an unusual practice of extracting from suppliers precise details on quality controls and speed of delivery, aiming always to buy from the best producer available. He also kept regular suppliers in close contact with their ultimate market by passing on information about customer preferences. Again, the procedures are so well ingrained in the company culture that new managers adopt them automatically.

The commitment to cleanliness and hygiene led Sainsbury to what were, for the time, open and airy shops, something which the company has followed ever since. When he died, John James Sainsbury's last words were, 'Keep the shops well lit.'

'The family influence on the company is small now,' says his great-grandson. 'But the founder influence is as strong as ever.'

The Marks & Spencer story is very similar. Michael Marks set a pattern of innovation in retailing when, as a young immigrant with a poor grasp of English, he competed with the raucous calls of other market traders by placing above his stall a large sign reading 'Don't ask the price; it's a penny'. Instead of selling whatever he could for as much as he could, Marks chose to sell the best quality he could find of as wide a range of goods as possible, all at one price. The goods were displayed in open baskets so customers could inspect them at leisure.

Other family members who took over the business added their own embellishments to this philosophy. Simon Marks and his brother-in-law Israel Sieff together introduced the concept of selling British which is so much part of the company's supplier concept today. Sieff's friendship with renowned scientist Chaim Weizmann in the 1920s established a perception of the value of new technology in helping suppliers to improve the quality and price of their goods. Simon Marks and Israel Sieff, too, were responsible for the remarkable reputation the company enjoys today for looking after the welfare of its staff and for involvement in community activities.

It is noticeable that even companies such as Racal, where the chief executive is not founder's kin – and indeed where family members of existing employees and directors are formally banned from joining the firm – still like to refer to themselves in family terms. 'Our family includes the employees and their wives,' says Harrison, somehow managing to make the statement sound anything but trite.

So what is it that the family or founder influence brings that contributes to the success of the business?

It seems there are at least four elements. Firstly, the founder and his family successors provide continuity. Says Lord Hanson: 'If you are involved in a family business, as one of the family, you accept responsibility early on. Training comes by osmosis; you can't help but absorb a

responsible attitude towards business.' A *Financial Times* profile described him as having been 'groomed to run his own business'. Even
now, there is a separate Hanson family business in which his own sons
are winning their spurs.

'It never occured to me to do anything else,' says Lord Sieff.

Sir Kenneth Cork had much the same experience and has observed
many family companies. 'I can't remember winding up a company
where the family was still there when it went broke,' he comments. The
family influence does not have to be obtrusive, he believes, pointing out
that 'nobody ever suggests there is nepotism in Barclays, which is a very
successful bank. There are about five families that came together from
different banks. Tim Bevan, the present chairman, is from one and Tony
Tuke, his predecessor, is from another.

'If you grow up in a family that runs a bank or a business, you learn
about it. It's sort of inbred. You hear about it at home, you learn to believe
in the company. I followed my father into an unusual business. I lived
with what happened in insolvencies, bankruptcies and liquidations.
My son does the same thing. You don't have to learn it – it's bred into
you.'

The Bulmer family owns 54 per cent of the cider firm's equity. 'Investment by the family is consistent,' says Nelson. 'That consistency is
present in all things, including, for example, marketing. They also have
a healthy desire for involvement in the company.' Most shareholders, he
points out, have neither the muscle nor the interest to become involved
in this way.

Secondly, they provide a long-term perspective and commitment
difficult for the professional manager from outside to assume. 'The founder takes a longer view than the professional manager,' says BOC's
Giordano.

Explains Forte: 'This cushion I am holding belongs about 20 per cent
to me. If someone drops it on the floor or mistreats it, I feel it.' How many
professional managers can say the same?

The fact that some professional managers do manage to take on the
same long-term perspective and commitment is a reflection that it is
possible in some cases for people to step into the founder's shoes.
Racal's Harrison, for example, is virtually the adopted business son of
founder Ray Brown. Harrison joined the company when he visited it to
audit the books. The young man so liked the look of the struggling little
firm that he never went back to his accounting job. In the early years,

before Brown left to take on a government job, Harrison absorbed the culture of the company so thoroughly that he became a natural successor and the transition passed almost unnoticed.

STC's Corfield presents a very different picture. Although he and Harrison have many similarities in their management style and approach, STC was not a young company when he joined. Its culture was strongly influenced by its transatlantic parentage. What Corfield has done is to create a new corporate culture within his part of the multi-national giant, a culture geared from the beginning to the possibility that the British company would one day be able to direct its own affairs, as indeed it eventually did. Whether STC could ever have bought itself out of ITT as a *successful* company without that change of culture is questionable. Corfield has, in effect, become that rare animal, a second-generation founder and one of those exceptions that proves the rule.

Thirdly, a family company has room for wider values than the norm. 'There's a lot more care in a family company,' maintains Lord Forte. Paternalism, sharpened with the grindstone of economic realism, can provide a very pleasant working environment. Part or whole ownership of the firm absolves the family chief executive of many of the guilt feelings that assail his typical professional counterpart when it comes to providing employee benefits. The family chief executive finds it easier to justify investments in employee wellbeing. This may explain why, contrary to normal expectation, executive turnover in successful family companies is often so low. The top executive teams of most of the companies in our sample have been remarkably stable, some lasting for twenty years and more. Yet conventional wisdom says that having a dynasty at the top creates a career blockage that forces out ambitious executives.

'Five co-directors started with me and all finished with me,' says Forte. 'There is actually *less* executive turnover in well-managed family companies.'

Fourthly, it is much easier for a family or founder company to establish a public identity that reinforces the brand image it wishes to portray. People have always been of more public interest than things. Says Forte: 'The family company is not faceless. It's not an anonymous someone who's burnt the bacon or provided good service – it's Charlie Forte who's done it!'

'A family company has character,' says a spokesman for Bulmer. What normal company would see in the obsolete railway tracks across its yards a perfect opportunity for a railway museum? The Bulmer family did, and earned themselves years of publicity for occasional trips on to the main line by Queen Victoria's royal coach and its steam engine. C.&J. Clark, too, with its Quaker background has a special character that is more than just paternal peculiarities. (These included ensuring, until recently, that the village pub in Street was dry.)

'In spite of our massive turnover and thousands of employees, no one in this company feels they are working for big business,' says Sainsbury's Dennis Males.

Against all of these advantages is the potential for disaster that comes from allowing incompetent family members to assume positions of responsibility. Most of our successful family companies seem to have overcome this by being more severe in their demands of family recruits into management than they are towards outsiders. Although there are an estimated 200 Clarks, Clothiers and other family members who could play a role in C.&J. Clark, most are weeded out at an early stage and promotion depends heavily on ability. At M&S, too, says Lord Sieff, 'A number of members of the family have come into the business and not made it.' It seems that the strength of Clark's culture is such that it automatically rejects those who do not fit the mould.

Edgar Schein of Massachusetts Institute of Technology's (MIT) Sloan School of Management has been looking at these issues through analysis of the behaviour and perceptions of founders of a variety of US firms. Schein begins from an assumption that culture emerges firstly from the beliefs and theories that founders bring to the organization and secondly from what the organization subsequently learns from experience.

Schein found that the personality of the founder was a key factor in culture creation: 'Some founders deliberately choose to build an organization that reflects their own personal biases while others create the basic organization but then turn it over to subordinates as soon as it has a life of its own. In both cases, the process of culture formation is complicated by the possibility that the founder is "conflicted", in the sense of having in his own personality several mutually contradictory assumptions.' For example, he may espouse the cause of delegation but actually keep interfering in trivial matters.

Founders create culture in a whole range of ways, from the design of office space and buildings, through organizational structure to how they recruit, select, promote and 'excommunicate' people. Schein observes, however, that the three principal ways they persuade other people to accept their concept of the right way to run the business are: 1) by deliberate role modelling, teaching and coaching people; 2) what they pay attention to; 3) how they react to critical events. These are the activities which have greatest effect in stamping the founder's model of the world on other people.

Schein found that 'the founder/owner is seen as being more self-oriented, more willing to take risks and pursue non-economic objectives and, by virtue of being the founder/owner more *able* to take risks and to pursue such objectives [than professional managers]. Founders/owners are more often intuitive and holistic in their thinking, and they are able to take a long-range point of view because they are building their own identities through their enterprises.'

He develops his argument by maintaining that founder/owners contain and absorb anxiety and risk in their organizations. The greater personal security and confidence they have compared with most professional managers means that they can provide an oasis of calm in times of crisis. 'They play a special role in reassuring the organization that it will survive,' says Schein.

Schein endorses the view that founder/owners can make humanistic and social concerns stick far more easily than can professional managers, and that founders are much more willing and able to innovate, because they are less constrained by the need to plan and document. Once all the planning and documentation is done, the founder/owner still has the option to follow his instincts and say, 'Yes, but we're going to do it anyway.'

The key to the long-term success of the family company is how well the original values that made the company can be inculcated in the following generations of managers (whether family or professional managers or both) and adapted to new circumstances. Each generation of employees or family members develops a new range of assumptions based on its own experiences. Explains Schein: 'Some of these new assumptions will solve problems better than the original ones because external and internal problems will have changed as the organization matured and grew. The founder often recognizes that these new assumptions are better solutions and will delegate increasing amounts of authority to those managers who are the best "hybrids"; those who maintain key old assumptions yet add relevant new ones.'

It is interesting to contrast this with events in one of Britain's largest publishing houses. The transition from one generation to the next was interrupted by handing over the reins to professional management, with the virtual abdication of the family next in line. While this worked well for a number of years, by the time it came to the transition to the next generation, the professional management, lacking the family's long-term vision and commitment, had run out of steam and the company had plateaued. The professionals were unable to seize and develop the family vision and culture; the further they departed from that culture, the more difficult it was to obtain commitment and growth. Significantly, a sudden opening for the return of the family to leadership of the company was seen by employees as a major opportunity to restore its flagging fortunes.

So the process of leadership by family or founder influence is at least partly a matter of handing down and adaptation. In each of our sample of companies, the successive generations of leaders have had sufficient insight into their own culture to guide the transition process. And that perhaps is as good a demonstration as any of effective leadership at work.

Of course, there are examples of successful companies where the family connection is extremely weak, or even, in Racal's case, actively discouraged. Sir Nigel Broackes, for example, has not sought to found a management dynasty at Trafalgar House and reportedly takes great pleasure in the fact that his son has chosen a completely different career – he is a philosophy don at Oxford!

11 Success versus failure

From the beginning of the *Winning Streak* project we were aware that it would not be enough merely to identify a number of common characteristics among successful firms. If unsuccessful companies also exhibited most or all of those same characteristics, it would be difficult to sustain the argument that they constituted a recipe for success. On the other hand, if the factors were frequently absent in companies that did not do well, then that was an indication that they did indeed constitute a winning streak.

To test the eight factors, we selected a small sample of manifestly unsuccessful companies. Some of these were in the turn-around phase and therefore more willing to talk about previous failings. A few were still deeply in trouble. We also drew upon published material, such as Sir Michael Edwardes' biographical account of his years at British Leyland, and several analyses of corporate collapse. Sir Kenneth Cork, the UK's best-known receiver and liquidator, and Ian MacGregor, formerly chairman of British Steel Corporation and now chairman of the National Coal Board were among the top executives who gave their time to the project. We were also able to draw upon the experience of Performance Analysis Services, a City firm specializing in the prediction and analysis of large company failure.

The upshot is that the unsuccessful firms all demonstrated a lack of some or most of the characteristics of success. Those such as Woolworth, British Steel, Ever Ready or British Leyland, which were on the way to recovery after energetic action at the top, have all pinpointed several of the characteristics as areas where improvement was needed and have invested considerable time and effort into making sure it happened. Those that were still on the downward path appeared to be paying little or no attention to several of these areas.

1. Leadership

There is little doubt that lack of effective leadership is a crucial factor in many sagas of company failure. The theme is echoed and re-echoed in all of the unsuccessful companies.

Michael Edwardes, for example, highlighted leadership as the critical problem at BL. Weak leadership, making frequent and damaging concessions in trade union negotiations, 'simply lost control of the situation'.

'When management down the line have their position undermined often enough through indecisive leadership,' he maintains, 'they give up the unequal struggle, and that is exactly what happened at British Leyland ... management over a number of years lost their will to manage.... "Management" is not an automatic right, it has to be earned. It is a duty, and if it isn't fulfilled it lets everyone down: employee, fellow manager, customer, supplier and shareholder.'

Woolworth, before the arrival of chairman John Beckett, was in a situation where any management team would have found it difficult to exert leadership. Explains executive director Nigel Whittaker: 'The company was 51 per cent owned by the US Woolworth. The US parent company was seen as a thorn in the flesh by the people here. It was drawing on the company through dividends, taking away money the British board wanted to use in the stores. The parent company restricted their freedom of action. It imposed controls but gave no leadership.

'The Americans saw the British as not knowing where they were going, failing to understand the proper relationship between the board and the shareholders, and not producing the results.'

One result of this was an acrimonious relationship with the press and the City. 'They were concerned about talking about what they were doing because they were afraid of being criticized. They became paranoic about analysts and journalists, so they didn't get a good press,' says Whittaker.

Another result, says Beckett, was that 'top management knew what had to be done, but could not bring itself to do it'. It is, says Richard Taffler of Performance Analysis, very common for the board of ailing companies to fail to grasp the nettle. Loyalties built up over the years make vigorous action very painful. It is to the credit of Woolworth's previous chairman that he recognized this and told the incoming team how much he envied them the opportunity to take a new broom to the company's operations.

Because leadership is so frequently at the heart of a troubled company's problems, a clean sweep at the top is often essential to put the show back on the road. Says Hanson Trust executive Dick Garrett: 'A badly managed company is like a boiled egg. You can't eat it till you've whipped the top off. Underneath there is usually some excellent management.'

Ever Ready is a typical example from the Hanson stable. Michael Johnson, now managing director of Ever Ready Ltd, was running an overseas subsidiary of the company in South Africa. Berec, as the Ever Ready group had been renamed, 'was a classic case of a company that had lost its way. It had grand international ideas for which the milch cows in the UK and South Africa paid the bill. Profit had dropped from £30 million to £10 million, while the British and South African operations were making £28 million profit. Senior management and middle management were very critical, but powerless to change matters. Obvious things were not being done, and the decision to change the brand name from Ever Ready, which everyone recognized, to Berec, which no one had heard of, seemed to be throwing away the value of a famous brand name,' says Johnson.

Hanson executive Tony Alexander won the backing of these managers by listening carefully to what they had to say, and backing them against the Berec board, who stayed in their posts for some months after the takeover. 'It was as if Hanson had sprayed them with insecticide,' says Johnson. 'They were laying there with their feet in the air, comatose but present.' Among the actions Alexander took was to bring back the Ever Ready name, restoring the identity of the company, and closing down the marginal and loss-making operations overseas. The worst of these was probably the West German subsidiary, where, says Johnson, 'the market was a bloodbath, the most competitive in Europe. Having built a new factory there, they found they couldn't close the old one.'

'It's our experience', says Lord Hanson, 'that in 99 per cent of troubled companies the [below-board] management there has not been given a chance to manage.'

Woolworth, too, found that middle management responded well to the change. Says Beckett: 'The takeover was clearly welcomed by a large part of the management cadre. They demonstrated a remarkable enthusiasm and a desperate wish for success. Almost the first thing I did was to meet a representative committee of store managers. It was the first time a chairman had ever seen a delegation of managers in that way. The fascinating thing was that although there had been a pretty autocratic style of management in the business before, they were ready to say what they thought was wrong and how it should be put right.'

The proposals boiled down to:

—For Christ's sake tell us who our boss is

—Get rid of the excessive bureaucracy

—Allow us to manage without too many people telling us what to do

—We accept there have to be redundancies, but select people on the grounds of age and incompetence and improve the terms

—Tell us what you want us to do and we'll get on with it.

At BSC, on the other hand, Ian MacGregor took a very different view. It was not at top-management level that leadership was lacking, but at government level, he concluded. 'My government mentors said I might have to clean up the management. I convinced the authorities I should take two months to look over the organization while Charles [Villiers] was there. I concluded there was nothing wrong with the people, who were well-trained and well-selected.

'I said: "Why not take that organization as I found it and help it succeed, and prove that British management was perfectly capable of matching any in the world? The only change I made at the top was to split finance and supply. Although I'd been cautioned management was not capable, I saw that the real problem had been a lot of intervention. So I reached an agreement with the Government that it would not interfere.'

Visible management The tale goes that Sir Campbell Fraser, former chairman of Dunlop, was refused entry by a doorman at a main office, because the functionary had no idea who he was. Whether true or not, there is little doubt that Dunlop top management failed to achieve an identity with the work force.

Comments John Simon, a former Dunlop managing director, who resigned in protest at the ill-fated and abortive merger with Pirelli: 'It was an autocracy throughout. Geddes [the chairman at the time of the merger] had a first-class academic brain but he simply couldn't communicate. There was always a barrier. His mind moved in a rarefied atmosphere. Thus there was no leadership. It was a faceless board, completely introverted. People who were entrepreneurial and could talk to the employees were never appointed to the board.'

Sir Kenneth Cork, who has witnessed a myriad of company demises, draws the contrast between founder/entrepreneurs who are known to the employees and professional managers who are not. 'Take old man

Handley Page, for example. He knew every workman, did the work himself and probably designed the aircraft. He was followed by professional management, who never, never communicated with the work force, had a lot of designers and accountancy personnel about the place – but there was no atmosphere, no feeling,' he explains. The absence of visible leadership divorced the people below from any aspirations top management may have had.

Ever Ready's Michael Johnson shakes his head as he recalls the only time he saw the Berec chairman in his last twelve months of office – 'and that was to complain that a battery he had bought had too much wax on it!'

Woolworth's chairman and chief executive were very visible in the field, says Beckett. But the authoritarian culture of the company made it difficult to extract full value from that visibility. No matter that they were close in the flesh, if people still felt them to be distant.

Clear mission Cork refers frequently to top management that has given up its essential role of setting realistic and imaginative goals for the business. Top management gets so bogged down in day-to-day matters that it stops thinking about the grand picture. 'When I go into businesses in trouble I find that the more troubled they are, the harder the chief executive works. Why does he work so hard? As an alibi for thinking. If he thinks, it gives him a pain in the stomach; he knows he's going broke and it's all dishonour and shame, so as an alibi for that he gets in early, he does everything the office boy should do, dictates letters, rings up people, works like hell and goes home at seven or eight o'clock at night saying: "I'm exhausted. Give me a gin." What he has done is stopped thinking for a day. I've a little saying: "If you've got a managing director who is busy, sack him." It's his job not to be busy, it's his job to put his feet on the desk, smoke his pipe and think – during office hours – whereas most people only think outside office hours.'

Woolworth's decline began in the 1950s and 1960s when profits were increasing. 'The board lost its way,' says Whittaker. 'The future was not being planned and important opportunities were being lost. The classic example was Woolco. It was the first out-of-town superstore chain. But they gave up the opportunity to become a large out-of-town food retailer. Woolco just became a large Woolworth.'

The problem goes back, Beckett suspects, to well before the time of the outgoing board. 'The tradition of Woolworth was to sell very large numbers of small items at 3d or 6d each. That was the basis of the business and it provided a focus not only to the manager and the buyer but throughout the organization. When they removed that discipline the company began to lose its focus both with the customers and with the employees.' Even so, it took a long time for the problem to catch up with the company – not until 1969 did M&S overtake Woolworth as the largest retail chain in profit and turnover.

Clear objectives MacGregor, in addition to giving the British Steel top management the freedom to get on and manage, put heavy emphasis on setting clear goals – something he immediately diagnosed as absent. 'I work on the same principle as people who train horses,' he says. 'You start with low fences, easily achieved goals, and work up. It's important in management never to ask people to try to accomplish goals they can't accept.'

2. Autonomy

Ian MacGregor, reported the *Observer*, 'prefers to test out the top management he inherits and give them more power if they can take it. With firm direction from the top, he makes a virtue out of administrative devolution, demanding that more and more decisions are taken down at the plants or the pits.'

MacGregor started his surgery at BSC by chopping the 1000-strong headquarters staff to 170 and moving them to a modest building on London's South Bank. Woolworth only had 500 people at its head office, but there were four regional headquarters, each with another 300 staff. 'It was terribly top-heavy,' says Whittaker. 'It was everyone's ambition to get out of the stores and into headquarters.' Now the company has eight small regional offices, each with twenty-five people, and a much reduced head office.

Ever Ready's headquarters of 250 people has been shrunk to 120, with an increase in effectiveness because the team was small enough for people to work closely together.

Almost all the unsuccessful companies have been characterized by an extensive bureaucracy and centralized operations. In Ever Ready's case, there were five tiers of management between the chief executive and the plant managers. Now there is only one. Rationalization at Woolworth led to redundancy for 550 of the company's 1250 middle managers. Increased redundancy payments and the knowledge that radical action was essential meant that the painful action was generally accepted.

Our successful companies fell into two types: those, primarily retailers, who were heavily centralized and those who were heavily decentralized. In both cases, the choice of which extreme to go to was based on clear management philosophies and understanding of the marketplace in which they operated. At the same time, whether centralized or decentralized, the successful companies made strenuous and largely effective efforts to minimize the bureaucracy. Central controls were only imposed where they were vital to the conduct of the business.

By contrast, the unsuccessful companies seem to have little clear concept of whether to centralize or decentralize. Most drift towards bureaucratic centralization because they feel more secure the more they can keep under their thumb. Trust is minimal.

Delegation all down the line The organizational structure in many unsuccessful companies makes it very difficult to delegate effectively. The National Coal Board, for example, was a mass of committees. It was, says MacGregor, a result of 'the long history of political intervention. The organization had to become defensive, so it developed an enormous number of committees. The NCB is dominated very heavily by committee, so no one knows who has made a decision. I'm busily dismantling them.'

In BSC, he recalls, 'The main barrier to leadership at lower levels was lack of confidence in management's sincerity in decentralizing and granting them authority. They were nervous of this new form of organization.'

Unfortunately, reports a former BSC manager, in some parts of the corporation the responsibilities that had been delegated under MacGregor have slowly but surely been pulled back since he left.

Much the same was true of the National Health Service, according to the Rayner report, which found that many decisions were either not made or were inoperable compromises, because the authority was never vested in an individual.

In such an environment, the individual becomes very unwilling to accept delegation even if it is offered, because it is not worth sticking his neck out.

Positive attitude towards risk-taking Risk-taking at Dunlop was rarely calculated, according to John Simon, who maintains that it happened more by caprice of the chairman than by any rational process. The involvement of other directors in the negotiations over the Pirelli merger was small, he claims. 'On one occasion,' he recalls, 'half of the Canadian company was sold by the Dunlop chairman on a whim while crossing the Atlantic. The company had to buy it back later.'

The problem was exacerbated by the understanding that no one interfered in another director's area of responsibility. To do so would have been regarded as the height of bad manners and would have attracted a furious repulse. Significantly, one of the first changes introduced by the new team at Woolworth's was exactly the opposite. Although each director has clear responsibilities and is expected to make the decisions in his functional area, everyone is encouraged to give comments and advice in each other's bailiwick.

Generalist managers Many unsuccessful companies are deeply suspicious of generalist managers. Promotion, particularly in many engineering companies, is primarily via functional channels and people are neither encouraged nor, in many cases, permitted to cross between them. On the other hand, it may be equally dangerous to populate a company with generalist managers who do not begin with a strong functional background to enable them to understand the fundamentals of the business they are in. The best of both worlds – in manufacturing industry at least – is probably to ensure that a high proportion of managers begin with a thorough technical knowledge and develop generalist skills. Our observations are that our very successful companies tend to make the transition to broader management skills early in the manager's career, while less successful companies may delay the transition until the manager's habits and way of thinking may be petrified with his narrow functional role. The research literature on this topic, as with so many of the aspects of management we have touched upon in *The Winning Streak*, seems to be lamentably thin.

3. Control

The problem with many unsuccessful companies is not that they have no controls. Rather it is that the controls they have are not used properly, or monitor the wrong things, or are buried in such mountains of data that critical problems simply fail to surface.

Our successful company chairmen insist that large amounts of useful data are gathered. But they rely on a small number of clearly defined measures to keep them informed as to where the company is going and how it is doing. At Woolworth, on the other hand, the board was deluged with forty-page detailed reports. These have now been scrapped in favour of one page of A4.

MacGregor, too, has had to fight a war on paper in both British Steel and the National Coal Board. He explains: 'The control systems here at the NCB are very complex. I'm trying to analyse what information is really necessary to monitor performance. The paperwork is stimulated by the Government's desire for statistical information. We are finding out why government needs more information about the business than the management does.'

Cork goes further: 'It used to be that there was a great shortage of paper in companies, in cash flows, profit forecasts and so on. People used to wait until the auditors turned up and then looked at the results with surprise .... Now I think it is the opposite – it is a glut of paper, all printed in silly little dots that you can hardly read, on the computer.

'When I go to a company to do an investigation, or to talk to the management, I ask them simple questions. What's your cash flow? When does it peak? What's your profit forecast? What's your turnover last week? And all they do is press a ruddy button and in comes an accountant with a pile of papers a mile high. Then they shuffle them and they can't find the right one.

'Nobody can think with a piece of paper. There's only one place you can think. A good businessman will answer all your questions out of his head.' All top management needs, he insists, is one sheet of paper.

The chief executive who needs vast amounts of information is in essence admitting that he has not got clear objectives. According to Cork, 'The only information you want is information on which you can make a decision. If you can't make a decision having read it, you don't want it. Some board meetings are full of "Well, I never" information.' Typical 'Well I never' information, he suggests, is 'We sent three wheelbarrows last month to Mexico.'

Tight limits on capital spending Most unsuccessful companies have tight limits on capital spending – because they don't have the cash to spend. Dunlop's Simon recalls signing in 1960 for a replacement for a compressor installed in 1912!

These limits do not seem to be imposed as part of a co-ordinated and effective effort to direct resources where they would have most effect. Rather they are permanent panic measures born out of the constant shortage of cash. When these businesses do have cash, they tend to spend it on the wrong things, because their control systems do not direct spending to the sharp end of the business. The large, central London headquarters of past and present unsuccessful companies (many of them now empty or tenanted by others) are a silent witness.

Some companies in trouble still do not tighten up on capital expenditure even when the writing is on the wall. At Ever Ready, for example, says Johnson, 'Capital spending was very lax. One of the first things Hanson Trust did was to put a stop to all capital spending for a while, on the basis that it did not know enough about the business to make spot judgements. People who really needed something had to fight for it.' As a result, the discipline of thinking through whether something was really needed, and of making a convincing case for it, quickly became ingrained in the Ever Ready management.

One of the classic modern examples of failure to keep control of cash flow was Laker. Although the circumstances surrounding the bursting of the bubble are still unclear, and will remain so until the long-term legal battles are cleared up, a more prudent management would probably not have permitted the company to become so exposed.

Close attention to business planning The effectiveness of stragetic planning depends to a large extent on the vision of top management, which gives the plan direction and shape. Unsuccessful companies *do* frequently make detailed plans for the future; but how strategic those plans really are is far more difficult to assess. In order to elicit clear differences between successful and unsuccessful firms in this respect, we felt it would be necessary to make very detailed studies comparing both the method and the content of the planning process. Again, this is a task for the future.

Long-term perspective Dunlop, says John Simon, 'had no long-term perspective. There was never any question, for example, of getting out of tyres.'

Woolworth's top management had no idea of how to develop their property portfolio as a long-term asset. It put twenty-five prime high street sites on the market at the same time, causing chaos in the property market and depressing the amount it received. No one had bothered to think about long-term disposal.

High standards Lack of standards contributed to most of the problems at Jaguar. As one motor trade magazine expressed the situation at Jaguar: 'Sales had slumped – and for a good reason. Bluntly, the product was not living up to its former reputation; reliability was poor, warranty bills had soared, customers complained of poor paintwork and indifferent service, and productivity was abysmal.' A major part of the solution was to impose much tougher standards on employees, suppliers and the dealer network. Over a two-year period, for example, Jaguar parted company with more than a hundred dealers who failed to reach new standards. Most others reacted to the company's quality campaign by tightening up their customer service.

At Woolworth, standards of service, where they existed, were neither generally understood nor applied. On the day the takeover was announced, one of the daily newspapers carried a cartoon in which a City businessman remarked to a colleague that he had tried to buy Woolworth ages ago, but could never find anyone to take the money! Hoover, another company with a far from exemplary profit performance, gained such a reputation for poor service and failure to answer customers' telephone calls for service, that it was joked that the initials stood for Hang On and On for eVER.

Lack of high standards goes back to a failure by senior management to communicate clear objectives. Standards do not exist in isolation; they have to be developed against a background of purpose. Without that, it is not surprising that what standards there were, were ineffective.

4. Involvement

Pride in ownership Unsuccessful companies appear in general to be slow in adopting employee share schemes. This may be a reflection of their forecast of future share-price involvement.

The unsuccessful companies are also, in general, not noted for their degree of employee participation. Although BSC, for example, was one of the first organizations in Britain to have a formal worker-director scheme, it was hardly a success and participation did not extend in any meaningful way to ordinary employees.

'Pride in ownership' had also been lost in many of the unsuccessful companies by abandonment of trade names that gave people their working identity. Ever Ready would have disappeared without Hanson intervention and one of the first steps Peter Harper took on taking over the UDS group was to give the stores back their traditional name of Allders. Restoring the name went a long way towards restoring the staff's self-confidence and general image of the company, he believes.

When Jaguar was renamed 'large car asssembly plant number one', its founder, Sir William Lyons, marched into the boardroom and removed his portrait from the wall. He had no intention of presiding, even on canvas, over the undermining of the principles of grace, pace and space on which he had built the company and its reputation.

John Egan, the sixth chief executive in eight years, describes what happened: 'In 1975 an attempt was made to subjugate Jaguar, along with other marques such as Rover, Land-Rover, Triumph, Austin Morris, MG and so on, under the ill-fated Leyland Cars umbrella.

'At one stage Jaguar flags at the entrance to the factory were torn down. Only Leyland flags were allowed to be flown on the premises and telephonists were threatened with disciplinary action if they answered callers with "Good morning. Jaguar Cars." Instead they were supposed to say, "Good morning. Leyland Cars," and if any further address was needed, "Large assembly plant number one." Worse still, the then two constituent factories of Jaguar were put into two quite separate organizational units within Leyland – the Power and Transmission Division and the Body and Assembly Division – hardly an appropriate fate for one of the most famous marque names in the world motoring industry.

'Sir Michael Edwardes' ... genius was to recognize immediately that no progress was possible unless famous marque names were re-created as a focus for group and individual loyalty.'

The same experience has been recorded at Allied-Lyons. In the late 1960s the then Allied Breweries made a major error, says chairman Sir Derrick Holden-Brown, when it listened to the advice of consultants and submerged all the names of the small breweries under one large company umbrella, with the unimpressive and uninspiring name of ABUK. Holden-Brown, then chief exeuctive of the Showerings, Vine Products & Whiteways Division, refused against considerable pressure to follow suit, a decision which, he says, did not make him popular at the time.

'In our division that would have meant losing company names such as Britvic, Harveys of Bristol and Coates Gaymers,' he says. 'We would have lost a vital element of our business life, the fact that people could say, "I work for Grant's of St James's or Wm Teacher."'

And that indeed is what happened in the beer division, where, says Holden-Brown, 'Everyone lost their way. Nobody wanted to work for this faceless company. It was not until 1978 that we could begin the process of re-establishing the true identity of these companies, and it took five years to get it really right, that people once again saw themselves as working for Benskins or Tetley Walker.'

The experience of unsuccessful companies tends to confirm the importance of giving employees a feeling that they can identify with their place of employment.

High pay or incentives Unsuccessful companies tend to be low payers. This does not seem to be by virtue of their economic circumstances; rather it is a lack of awareness of the motivating influence pay and incentives can have. The top management of family companies, far from being pinch-penny as the popular image would suggest, are often so closely involved with the profitability of the organization themselves that they have to understand the tie between effort and reward.

At BSC, says MacGregor, 'I put as many people as possible on pay programmes that reflected their performance. I had an enormous struggle over that.' Part of the problem, he explains, was convincing civil servants that people in state-owned industry could possibly be worth more pay than they themselves were getting.

Promotion from within Our successful companies had a strong reliance on promotion from within and saw this as a way of strengthening the cultural characteristics that they wanted to preserve. So, too, do many unsuccessful companies. The difference appears to be that the successful companies are continually building upon the company culture, adapting it to the real world, while the unsuccessful companies tend to choose for promotion people who will freeze the company culture.

The experience of Woolworth shows how detrimental total reliance on promotion from within can be in those circumstances. Management in the company was entirely inbred, says a stockbroker specializing in the retail sector. Management was derived from people who joined at school-leaving age with poor qualifications. They began 'sweeping the stockroom floor'. The best store managers became buyers. The best buyers became senior managers. There was a concern about people who were 'too clever'. It all led to a management organization that was inward looking and lacked confidence. Beckett was the first chairman not to have started by sweeping the floors.

Dunlop, too, had a high reliance on promotion from within, although instead of a bias against people who were too clever, it went to extremes in hiring Oxbridge graduates, says Simon. The result was that people were set in the same mould before they even arrived in the company. The lack of diversity of background must have contributed considerably to the company's blinkered view of the outside world.

High degree of communication Woolworth was characterized by an abundance of information where it wasn't needed and an autocratic management style that left employees with little idea of what was expected of them. One of the first actions of the new management was to institute a whole range of communications methods, including interdisciplinary task forces, mass meetings and an internal newspaper aimed at keeping managers informed of what was happening and planned.

Hanson's acquisition of Allders revealed a caucus of managers eager to act but poorly informed as to the objectives they were working to. 'We brought the managers into our plans, stressing that whatever happened, this was to become a strong unit on its own,' says Hanson. All the managers needed was to be kept regularly informed.

Stress on training Some of the unsuccessful companies do pay strong attention to training. The training function may even be highly efficient. But there exists a question mark over whether it is also effective in terms of the company's overall objectives. In other words, does it deal with future needs in a planned and consistent manner? If the company does not have a clear mission and a commonly understood and accepted set of objectives, then the best training efforts may go to waste. This, we suspect, is what happens in many unsuccessful companies.

It is significant that several of the successful companies have gradually moved their management training function away from general courses towards highly specific courses aimed at meeting individual managers' development needs. Various forms of distance learning play a part here, with the revived British Leyland among the leaders in developing practical methods.

151

Does this mean then, that stress on training is not on its own a significant factor in business success? A lot more research would be needed to prove this one way or the other. But some indications may be gained from examining the case of British Shipbuilders. Attempting to discuss with the state company the reasons for the British shipbuilding industry's doldrums elicits an outpouring of excuses. It has been hit by 'unfair competition', 'cheap labour', or 'recalcitrant unions'. Yet other industries have met the same difficulties and not only survived, but prospered. Some independent shipyards, too, have a much better-than-average record of profitability and competitiveness. If we delve a little deeper, we may lay the blame on poor management, which failed to invest in the future because it failed to develop meaningful objectives and strategies, and which failed to provide the leadership necessary to muster all resources of the yards to a common end.

Comparing the British yards with their Japanese counterparts certainly suggests that all these failings were there. But the comparison also throws up one other stark contrast. The Japanese yards were and still are staffed by relatively highly qualified personnel. They invest heavily in training to ensure that their labour force at all levels understands what is required of them. The British yards, on the other hand, were characterized by a poorly educated work force, most of whose training took place under old-fashioned apprenticeship schemes, where knowledge was passed on from a hoary old hand whose status often depended on delaying as long as possible the time when other employees reached his level of skill.

Social side of work It may seem strange, but reinstating a social programme was one of John Egan's priorities at Jaguar. Egan recognized that a work force which had been uninvolved could be revitalized if the whole family were brought into the company's struggle to survive and prosper. In addition to the regular quarterly videos presented to employees in groups of 200 to 300, highlighting progress and areas of production difficulty, he reinstated a number of traditional events that had been lost in the years when the Jaguar identity was suppressed. Among these were family nights, where friends and relatives of employees could hear about the company's progress and its future plans; open days for families to see what working in the factory was like (attended by 25,000 people), and a whole series of events such as bonfire night celebrations, mini-marathons and pantomime visits.

It is not difficult to think of companies which have been through severe ups and downs, and yet maintained a relatively active social life and an ability to add enjoyment to working hours. Dunlop, too, even by John Simon's account, was 'an easy-going, happy family'.

Other unsuccessful companies clearly do not put much effort into creating an environment where people can enjoy being at work. Successful companies that do not pay much attention to this area can fall back upon the stimuli of growth and opportunity, which in themselves create job satisfaction. Unsuccessful companies cannot.

Genuine respect for the individual Unsuccessful companies may also be caring companies. Both Dunlop and BSC have been in the forefront of organizations dealing humanely with redundant employees. BSC has invested tens of millions of pounds in job creation efforts, aimed at replacing some of the jobs lost in plant closures in areas where alternative employment is hard to find. Dunlop is one of the few companies to experiment with linked subcontracting, where redundant employees are hired back part time as independent operators.

At Woolworth there was a prevailing attitude that 'the business was there to see that the employees were OK'. However, this attitude led to all kinds of abuses and tolerance of second-rate performance.

But does the absence of respect for individuals actually breed company failure? All the management literature would suggest that it reduces the capacity for involvement, by alienating people, by preventing them identifying their own goals with those of the company.

If the greatest respect a manager can show to a subordinate is to listen to him, then many unsuccessful companies would fail the respect test. Says Cork: 'When I go into a [troubled] company and ask for some information, it is very unlikely that the managing director has got it. But somewhere there is George who does know. George is dying to tell somebody, but no one will listen to him. If the management had actually talked to George, then the company would have fared much better. When we go in [as receivers] we use George. When we have successes, it's really George who has them. We wouldn't know what to do.

'Willy Stern, for example, had below him some very good people. But Willy had this enormous imagination and was convinced he was God's gift to the property world, and so he never listened to them.'

5. Market orientation

When Michelin brought out its radial tyre, Dunlop's technical director declared that it was only a marketing gimmick.

Failure to understand or change with the marketplace is a frequent cause of company collapse. It was, for example, one of the principal reasons for the débâcle of Cyril Lord's carpet empire, according to Dr A.F.L. Deeson's description of the decline and fall of Lord's empire. Says Deeson: 'In addition to all his other problems Lord had to face up to the fact (but failed to do so) that the carpet market was beginning to change. Nearly ten years before, Lord had confounded his competitors by using a new method of carpet manufacture and exploiting the economic and technical advantages by dynamic and unusual marketing. Now the competitors were coming back, exploiting a shift in public taste away from the flat "unsculptured" carpets by Lord towards the more elaborate Axminster-type designs.'

Lord failed to match the competition on price and pushed his own sculptured product on to the market with ill-considered haste, only to find that the product was so poor it had to be withdrawn, after costly compensation to aggrieved customers. This was the turning point in the company's fortunes, which even massive advertising campaigns could not restore (proving the dictum that all the advertising in the world won't sell a rotten product more than once).

Brand strength Companies in decline have frequently failed to maintain the strength of their brand names. Remarkably, it often takes very little real effort to restore the value of the brand name. Marmalade manufacturer Keiller, for example, which had been driven into severe losses by insufficient support from parent company Nestlé, is now thriving under a new management willing and able to make full use of the brand's image of quality and reliability.

Where the brand name is also the company name, failure to support it all too often amounts to failure to support the company – hence the examples of Ever Ready and Jaguar.

Marketing consultant Hugh Davidson has a fund of examples, where companies have confined themselves to being also-rans in their industry through failure to create a viable brand image. 'Littlewoods' retail store operation has been a consistent problem for them,' he says. 'They don't have a clear reason for being. They are low price but there are other places where you can buy cheaper. They have never established who they are and what they stand for. International Stores has the same problem and is steadily losing market share. Among the three mail-order firms who are not market leaders, only one is surviving well, and that is because it has developed its own image of being young and fashionable.'

One of the biggest follies of all, he suggests, was Distillers, who 'withdrew Johnny Walker Red Label from the UK market because of a row with the Common Market and tried to replace it with a new brand. They should have known that it takes twenty years to establish a new brand of whisky.'

Swift and comprehensive dealing with complaints Complaints-handling was a problem at both Jaguar and Woolworth, with Woolworth's Beckett now placing great emphasis on Marks & Spencer-style, no-questions-asked return of cash. The catalogue of company calamities at Performance Analysis reads like a *Who's Who* of indifference to customer problems, with notable exceptions such as Rolls-Royce, whose failure could almost be attributed to going overboard in keeping the customer happy.

Emphasis on quality control The lesson of Jaguar is already clearly documented. Jaguar, which had virtually no employee involvement in quality matters, now has sixty quality circles, covering almost every aspect of the business. 'It was abundantly clear from the onset', said Egan at the Institute of Directors' annual convention in 1984, 'that emphasizing quality as the number-one priority of the company met with the full approval of the work force.'

Failure to exercise efficient quality control does not seem to have caused many swift failures. But it has caused many slow deaths. Our unsuccessful companies, on the whole, do not seem to have had anything that could be described as a quality fetish. Their cultural perceptions do not accord quality the exceptional priority that so many of our most successful companies do.

Hunger for market information Jaguar had very little information on the extent of its problems, nor on its competitive status compared with its rivals in the luxury car market. Egan began with market research to establish where the company stood. Now the company conducts regular interviews with a hundred customers each month on both sides of the

Atlantic, checking whether they are fully satisfied with the vehicle, and, equally importantly, with the service they received from the dealer. The customer is re-surveyed at intervals, to ensure his satisfaction does not fall with experience.

Lack of market information – or at least the ability to interpret the information that was available – should have led TI, then Tube Investments, to think twice about its ability to compete with multinational competitors in the aluminium business. Although British Aluminium made hefty contributions to TI's profits in 1977, leading the engineering company to raise its stake in BA to 58 per cent, the first major downturn in the market left TI holding a very expensive baby. It cost TI more than £50 million in write-offs and losses to get rid of its aluminium interests.

Woolworth had excellent analyses of the market. Yet some inborn hubris prevented it from making use of it. Reports to Woolworth 'just gathered dust' says a management consultant.

Market-oriented research and development At Dunlop, claims Simon, 'We let R&D people do their own thing. There was little direction.'

Michael Edwardes recalls as long ago as 1957 the frustration of not being able to persuade British Leyland to make minor adaptations in its vehicles to meet operating conditions in Africa. The failure of BL's marketing function to provide a lead for research and development weakened it against more market-conscious competition, he believes. Edwardes upgraded the research and development facilities of BL, creating BL Technology Ltd, 'a central technical facility, but one largely directed by the operating companies towards meaningful market-related work'.

6. Zero basing

The most common statement as to why an established company has failed is that 'it lost its way'. In other words, it forgot the business it was in, or lost sight of the fundamental principles of that business.

Sticking to the last Cork recalls how, when Handley Page couldn't build aeroplanes, it decided to build a brewery in Turkey. 'What they had forgotten was that even when they had built it there was exchange control in Turkey and they couldn't get the money out. Another company in the motor industry for some reason bought a brickmaking machinery plant in the north. It nearly broke them . . . . The whole of their management effort was not in their business but trying to rescue a bankrupt brickmaking machinery factory . . . . If you want to get into something else you want to put your toe in and find out what it's like, not go and buy a business.'

Attention to detail At Woolworth disciplines were notably absent in many key areas of the business. For example, the store managers used to display their goods how they liked. Now detailed studies identify the best way to display each kind of goods and the store managers are obliged to keep to standard presentations.

Keeping the eye on the ball Unsuccessful companies have usually not been able to see clearly where they were going wrong – if they had, they would have taken action sooner. They tend to hang on to their mistakes well beyond the time needed to demonstrate that a mistake has truly been made. By waiting until an issue becomes critical, they wait too long. The directors of Jaguar knew that quality was fundamental to the success of their business and that quality was suffering, yet they took no firm action. The board of Woolworth knew that customers had a very poor opinion of the stores, yet took no positive action to change the quality of goods or service. Instead they tried to tackle the image through advertising 'the wonder of Woolworth's' – and simply made worse the contrast between what the customer felt he ought to find and what was really there.

We were not, as a result of our interviews, able to draw any particular conclusions as to the role of the non-executive directors in ensuring that the company does keep its eye on the ball. It seems that the non-executives at Dunlop were singularly ineffective, and this is probably true at many other unsuccessful companies. It also emerges that the chairmen of our successful companies by and large hold their non-executive directors in high esteem. Rocco Forte, for example, is fully aware of the steadying influence of long-serving non-executive directors of Trusthouse Forte.

However, the choice of non-executive directors, and the role they play, must influence a company's direction, if only in the sense that the company without an active and vocal non-executive voice on the board has no counterbalance to whatever whims and misreadings of the environment top management may indulge in.

It is significant that MacGregor, in creating his board at British Steel, separated the board from line management and pulled in non-executive directors to emphasize its overseeing role.

7. Innovation

There seems little doubt that failure to innovate, even in a mature industry, is a recipe for disaster. TI Raleigh, which once had 75 per cent of the British bicycle market, is a good example of a company that hardly innovated at all, depending on sales of basic models to developing countries. Exports to other Western countries plummeted and sales in the UK halved, against its implacable opposition to new forms of retailing. Only by massive spending on new designs and new production equipment has the company begun to recapture its lost market share.

Other examples abound. Where have all the pre-World War Two competitors of Sainsbury gone? Why did EMI falter? (Even when it created a world-beating product, it was unable to market it effectively and gave away the lead to overseas competitors.) Why is it that some companies fail to innovate when their survival depends upon it?

Absence or removal of barriers to change The centralized, ivory tower research and development laboratory is a recipe for innovation failure. Even if brilliant new products emerge, they are likely to meet the 'not invented here' reaction from sales and marketing.

Natural curiosity 'Not invented here' can also apply to ideas from outside the company – indeed, it is these ideas that usually suffer most. John Beckett describes the symptoms as 'hubris – the overweening self-confidence that, whatever the size or location, a company's tried and tested formula will continue to work'.

Dr Eddie Veyes, chief executive of Rylands Whitecross, has been busily turning round the wire company for several years. When he arrived, he recalls, he was struck particularly by the absence of innovation or even awareness of technical developments elsewhere. He realized how serious this was, he recalls, 'the first time I tried to hold a brainstorming here. There was no storm. There was no response, no to-ing and fro-ing of ideas.'

International perspective Unsuccessful companies do often have subsidiaries overseas, although these may be more of a drain than a benefit.

Cork points out that numerous companies have made abortive overseas acquisitions and investments which have brought them close to the edge, simply because the reasons for going abroad were inadequate. Very often, for example, it is a point of pride to be international – but pride goes before a fall. Cork describes 'one big firm of canners we dealt with, that ran extraordinarily successfully as long as the [founder] lived in this country. Then he decided to live abroad and to justify that he had a factory built abroad too. Once his hand was lifted off there was no other management.'

The point seems to be that just having overseas operations does not necessarily mean that a company will be internationally minded. Research by Harvard University's Prof. Michael Porter indicates that multinational firms with a global perspective perform on average better than those whose attention is focused securely on the home country.

Directed research and development The following example, from a study by Andrew Robertson of the Polytyechnic of Central London, rams home the point. Writing in *Chief Executive* magazine, Robertson records:

> Gauging Systems, the manufacturer of an electronic bottle scanning machine, was one of many thousands of companies that fell into this trap [the pursuit of the 'better mousetrap'] and paid the penalty. Its management assumed that a new method of detecting impurities in opaque liquids would be welcomed by dairies and other bottling plants, which were worried about the infringement of public health regulations. What it overlooked was that complaints were rare and the average fine around £100.
>
> On top of this, the company did not understand the conditions under which its device would have to work. It knew the speed of bottling – around 1000 an hour – but not that the line was hosed down after every shift. The snag was that the 9000 machine was not waterproof.

The role of the chief executive St Gallen's Cuno Pümpin tells the tale of one company where failure to remove the chief executive precluded any chance of moving the company in the cultural direction it had declared it wanted to go. He explains: 'One major Swiss company, with sales of several billion dollars, has a chief executive who is finance oriented, as is the company itself. He knows nothing about technology. He goes to sleep in meetings where technology is mentioned. Yet as soon as costs are talked about, he wakes up and takes part in the discussion.'

That company wanted to become innovative to expand its international activities. Several years later, nothing had changed, because other senior managers took their cue from the top.

8. Integrity

Integrity is not a word that figures strongly in the vocabulary of the unsuccessful companies. At Woolworth it was perceived as a major problem – far greater than it actually was, in fact. Blunt, unmisunderstandable statements from Beckett and action upon new 'draconian' rules removed the few real abuses there were and tightened up the whole attitude within the company.

Towards employees 'You have to project the image that you are honest in what you say,' says MacGregor. None of the unsuccessful companies we examined set out to be dishonest with their employees. But their lack of clear objectives, and standards to measure people by, meant in many cases that they couldn't ensure that people knew where they stood, nor could they be consistent in their behaviour towards employees.

A low employee perception of the company's fairness tends to be associated with a poor opinion of top management. At BL, for example, the unions' and the shop-floor employees' experience of top management had led to a mental picture of people who didn't know where they were going, nor were particularly worried about the consequences to the labour force. Michael Edwardes was able to make sweeping reductions in employee numbers, with minimal industrial relations problems, simply because it was accepted at all levels that he knew what he was doing and aimed to be fair. Ian MacGregor, too, was able to persuade the steel unions of his personal integrity and to use that as a starting point for saving as much as was economically viable of the industry. While they often disagreed with him, the union representatives were obliged to respect him.

Customers Both successful and unsuccessful companies refer instinctively to Marks & Spencer as the company to copy in terms of customer satisfaction. The difference is that the successful ones manage to adopt some or all of this aspect of the M&S philosophy, while the unsuccessful ones simply fail to get the message across at the customer interface, where it counts.

'The customer was a nonentity as far as BSC were concerned' says MacGregor. 'It was a long, difficult problem. There had been a shortage of steel in the mid 1970s, so it was a seller's market. BSC shied away from difficult specifications. It abdicated from the North Sea, for example, by avoiding the speciality steels. Now it is a lot more customer and service conscious.'

Suppliers Jaguar, when it analysed the causes of customer complaints, compiled a list of 150 areas of faults. Some 60 per cent of them turned out to be caused by faulty components from suppliers. One month the company returned 22,000 components to different suppliers. Jaguar suppliers now have to sign a contract that sets a maximum level for faults. If they exceed the quota, they have to pay for all the costs of putting it right, whether this means simply supplying a replacement for faulty components discovered before the parts reach the line, or repairing the car once it is in service. 'This seems to concentrate the mind remarkably,' says Egan.

Suppliers were also brought on to the multi-disciplinary task forces Egan established to tackle each of the common faults. The task forces had the simple objective of finding the fault, establishing and testing a cure, and implementing it as fast as possible. Jaguar directors chaired the task forces of the twelve most serious faults, but in one case the task force was chaired by the supplier's representative.

P.S. Sir William Lyons' portrait is now hanging proudly again at Jaguar.

Conclusion

The previous pages have examined a multitude of facets of a sample of Britain's most successful companies. We cannot guarantee that any company that follows the behaviour patterns of those companies will automatically succeed; but we are convinced that its chances will be improved. The eight factors are an excellent starting point for the company that wishes to create its own winning streak.

What those companies have to say about their culture, their behaviour and their attitudes raises a host of questions as well as answers. Some of these questions, such as the role of the family in preserving cultural continuity will, we hope, be investigated further by universities and business schools. Other questions that demand further study include:

Can corporate culture be changed?

If the sample of companies we have examined is anything to go by, the answer has to be yes. In the long-established companies, the culture is constantly evolving, with each generation making its mark. Although it carries many of the basic tenets of its founder, and would still be recognizable to him, the culture of a Sainsbury or a Marks & Spencer today has moved with the times to reflect modern values, modern challanges. In many of the younger companies, the culture is not yet fully formed. MFI and Asda, to stick with retailing examples, have both reached a point in their evolution where they recognize that a new set of values is needed to maintain impetus. MFI, which sold at first on price and the peculiar satisfaction that most men gain from pointing to self-assembled furniture and saying 'I did that', is now emphasizing quality. It is using key elements of the established culture, such as its innumerable incentive schemes, to change attitudes and perceptions at the operating level. Asda is now sinking great effort into progressively moving the culture away from high pressure and autocracy towards delegation and participation.

That organizations can change their culture radically is demonstrated by numerous examples in the UK and elsewhere. The story of Jaguar in recent years is a prime example of a company whose culture changed swiftly and for the worse as it lost its identity and sense of direction – only to reappear when those qualities were restored.

How to go about changing company culture is a matter for another book. But the following guidelines are suggested by what we have learned from our successful British companies:

- First, identify the culture you have. Perceptions may differ between functional departments or between levels of the hierarchy. If they do differ, you already have a problem of organizational identity, and cannot expect to make adequate use of the resources available to you until you obtain a unity of perception.
- Second, identify what kind of culture best fits the markets you operate in. Consider particularly who buys the product and whether cost or quality is the key criterion in the buying decision. This automatically tells you where you want to be and, by comparison with where you are, provides a pretty clear idea of the degree of change you need to make.
- Third, consider what organizational changes have to be made to accommodate any change of culture. The severity of these changes will depend closely on the gap between the desired and actual culture.
- Fourth, consider what personnel changes must be made. The place to start is at the top. Is the current top-management team willing and capable of displaying the kind of leadership by example that will convince people below of the need for change? It is of no value for top management to issue edicts if it does not follow them up with continued, unequivocal and uncontradicted action. Culture changes happen as people observe behaviour and attitudes that work, and assimilate them into their own ways of thinking and doing.

One of the strengths of many of the company leaders we have featured in this book has been their ability to adapt their own behaviour to stimulate cultural change. This is perhaps the hardest task of all.

163

Does the shape and composition of the board influence success?

Surprisingly little is known, in research terms, of what really goes on at board meetings. Few academics are privy to the top-level boardroom, while few executives have the qualifications or the time to conduct an analysis of boardroom behaviour. We have, however, been struck by the high value the companies in our sample of success place upon their non-executive directors, who are not mere figureheads, but active advisers.

The company without non-executive directors runs the constant risk of missing the blindingly obvious, but fatal, misdirection in its strategy and operations. It is unlikely that Laker, for example, would have become so exposed if active non-executive directors had been there to counsel caution and to keep the entrepreneur's feet on the ground.

The degree to which non-executive directors can contribute depends first, on their capability and suitability and second, on the degree of independence of view brought about by the manner of their appointment. The right board structure will ensure that the proper distinctions between the direction of the company and its management are maintained. Non-executive directors within such a structure can ensure that the board acts as a board and not as an extension of management – something in which Ian MacGregor, for one, is a passionate believer.

Pertinent to our success factors are the board's roles in appointing the chief executive, determining the businesses to be in or to discard, setting the standards of employee relations and quality assurance, challenging the technology, approving strategy and monitoring performance. The board can broaden the parameters within which decisions are made and ensure that major policy decisions are properly constructed and presented.

In these and so many other ways, the well-constructed board can provide the necessary backing to the company's leadership and ensure that the management is properly rewarded for success. To operate without an effective board may work for a while, but the continuity of success is inevitably at risk. The single entrepreneur may win for a while, but fail to hand on the recipe for success when he goes – particularly because entrepreneurs are often not very good at growing new entrepreneurs beneath them.

How important is an attitude of winning?

How often has a company's success been explained away with: 'They just happened to be in the right place at the right time!'? Ian MacGregor (who, when asked how he comes to be so hale and hearty in his seventies, replies, 'Choose your parents carefully; it's in the genes') insists that 'the first ingredient of success is luck – don't knock it!'

Yet if there is a single characteristic which is found in all of our successful companies, in most cases to an outstanding degree, it is the overwhelming commitment to winning. BOC's Giordano puts it this way: 'What else is there but winning? If you lose, you lose out!'

'You have to hate being a loser!' adds GrandMet's Grinstead.

Our successful companies make their own luck by their determination to win. The winning streak comes automatically to them, because their culture will allow for nothing else.

For the practising manager, our observations – which in essence are not ours but those of the top managers who run the successful companies – should help in the establishment of a practical framework for the improvement of his own company. We would like to think that they might also help some companies heading for disaster to pull back from the brink in time.

For the academic, it should provide a starting point for more intensive analyses of key issues, such as the role of the family or founder in long-term business success or the mechanism of effective centralization and decentralization. We don't pretend to have provided many answers in these contexts. Rather, we have raised questions that the academic community is best poised to answer – and we look forward with interest to the detailed research that we hope will be undertaken.

For the general reader, the trade unionist, the civil servant and the politician, we hope we have provided an insight into how successful businesses see themselves. The positive outlook, the ambition shared at many levels, the vitality of these companies, provide lessons from which all sections of the community can learn.

Appendix 1 The winning streak in smaller companies

by Peter J. A. Herbert

'Every day its own miracle!' These are the words used by David Gration, chief executive of a £2-million joint venture between Boots and Celltech, describing life as a front-runner in the fast-emerging field of diagnostic biotechnology – where one of his products alone has a worldwide market potential of £1 billion per annum! Is small *really* so beautiful? If so, then how do we account for the motives and skills which explain the existence of Sainsbury, Racal and our other winners? Are the ingredients for success the same in smaller companies as in their very large counterparts? How does the capacity to manage spectacular growth rates emerge? By accident, design . . . or by copying the styles and poaching the talents of the corporate élite of the day? Do we see £10-million or £50-million private companies run by irascible power-mongers with a beady eye for accounting ratios, by flamboyant entrepreneurs with a singular flair for selling, or by MBAs armed with every trick in the managerial conjuring box?

The purpose of this chapter is to examine whether the traits of success in our large companies can be observed in their smaller brethren, these being companies which were scarcely visible perhaps ten years ago but whose growth may have taken them to sales approaching £100 million. We are thinking not of business start-ups but rather of companies now employing several hundred people, which have grown and will grow very rapidly. Our aim is to see whether these companies exhibit the same perceptions of leadership, innovation and the like as we have already found or, if they do differ, whether they do so merely in degree rather than substance.

What, then, is the basis of the views to come? For the most part, the observations and conclusions are derived from visits and discussions with the management teams of smaller companies short-listed for the Business Enterprise Awards 1980 to 1983. Surprising though it may be, in an era of major structural shifts towards the service industries, the majority of these businesses are rooted in manufacturing consumer products, such as wall coverings, women's fashionwear, and fizzy drinks. There are also examples from sectors such as food re-

166

tailing and industrial cleaning. Further variety is to be found in geographical location, several cases emerging phoenix-like from the industrial wastelands of the north. Some of these high-fliers are already publicly quoted whereas others are privately owned and biding their time before succumbing to the tantalizing prospect of the 'bright lights'. Some are run by charismatic individuals although others, as we shall see, thrive on the leadership of complementary duos. But they all have one thing in common – a predilection to stand up and be counted against the mighty. Though not a prescription for success in itself, this combative tendency is an important manifestation of a deep-rooted ambition to outwit and outpace their rivals.

In the next few pages we shall examine this desire to excel in terms of our eight characteristics.

1. Leadership

In their recent book, *Managing Growing Organizations*, Theodore D. Weinshall and Yael-Anna Raveh argue for the orderly sequence of three forms of managerial structure through which organizations proceed in the course of growth and maturation. Initially, the small, young but fast-developing business must be managed by an informal, centralized organization with an 'entrepreneurial structure'. As growth accelerates, the number of managers required increases to the point where the entrepreneur can no longer even remember their names. Once this happens then the number of managers reporting directly to the entrepreneur must be reduced, their jobs thoroughly defined and a formal and centralized structure must be introduced with sufficient hierarchical levels. Further growth, when coupled with expanding product ranges and geographical dispersal, ultimately calls for formally decentralized methods of organization. Fairly orthodox stuff, but these authors go on to advocate that different types of leader are required when stability and growth, respectively, are the order of the day: stiffness and rigidity are needed in the first case, but flexibility in the second.

How can smaller companies cope? One solution appears to come from recognizing that entrepreneurs can come in pairs. At S.R. Gent – a fashionwear supplier to M&S whose turnover has climbed from virtually zero to over £70 million in fifteen years – Peter Wolff and Peter Wetzel have worked from the outset as joint chief executives. Whereas the former has concentrated on design and merchandising, the latter has specialized in production and manufacturing technology. Their personalities appear similarly complementary, and whilst one thrives on the volatility of the marketplace, the other looks to the quality and efficiency of production processes.

Similarly, at Iceland Frozen Foods – the thrusting rival to Bejam created by two disillusioned management trainees from Woolworth – Malcolm Walker and Peter Hinchcliffe have also found virtue in sharing the burden of leadership.

As joint chief executives, the first is at home with strategic planning and external relations, deferring to the operating strengths of his partner.

Of course, there is no guarantee that these alliances will survive. Indeed, the cynics are certain to argue that the lust for absolute power is sure to be latent in one or other member of such duos and that sooner or later the more conventional chairman and chief executive arrangement must emerge. Only time will tell! Certainly there is evidence that leaders can come in pairs and that they need not self-destruct before spectacular progress has been achieved.

Leaders are visible David Evans – ex-professional sportsman and now chairman and chief executive of Brengreen Holdings, a keen rival to Pritchard – urges to the effect 'who needs PR agencies if you give journalists a fair crack of the whip?'. This approach to public visibility has resulted, for example, in extensive media coverage of his company's vanguard attempt to privatize service facilities on one of British Rail's London commuter routes. Nevertheless, he is also very conscious of the need for visibility inside the company, even to the extent of riding refuse vehicles.

A similar pattern is revealed in all of our smaller winners. Stephen Bingham, who has led Sodastream from an all but defunct supplier of carbonated water dispensers to the aristocracy in 1973 to a worldwide market leader ten years later, walks the factory shop floor as if defying any employee to talk on other than Christian name terms. More formality exists at Iceland, but there's only one canteen and Malcolm Walker is not averse to joining the lads in their huge cold store – in shirt sleeves if that is what it takes!

At Gent, Peter Wolff shows no reluctance (indeed, quite the opposite) to immerse himself in the frenzied task each Wednesday night of getting 250 new designs of women's and children's garments made up and costed before he and his team set off from Barnsley to present their latest range to M&S buyers in London first thing the following morning. It is readily apparent that the effect of such visibility and activity permeate through the entire organization, so galvanizing it that sheer momentum seems destined to overrun any obstacle to success.

But a word of warning to those aspiring leaders seeking visibility as a prescription for motivating their peers and subordinates. Even in smaller companies striving to rank amongst the best, their leaders are energetic to the point of being peripatetic, obsessively enthusiastic about their products and people, engagingly iconoclastic and . . . physically conspicuous by being either very tall and slim or short and stocky.

What of the founder/family factor? None of our successful smaller companies are family businesses in the accepted sense. In part this is due to their comparative youth. For practical purposes all of them began on the road to their eventual success in the early 1970s. None have been faced with critical succession problems, for their leaders are relatively young, many being in their thirties or forties. Perhaps some of these companies will eventually come to be identified by their founders in the manner of Sainsbury or Marks & Spencer. But it seems unlikely. None carry the names or acronyms of their founders or de facto leaders. Both Brengreen Holdings and S.R. Gent are corporate names acquired as much by accident as design, bearing no obvious relationship with either their leaders or their products. The corporate identities of Iceland Frozen Foods and Soda-stream are plainly to be found in their products rather than their leaders. But this is not to gainsay the existence of distinctive managerial cultures in these companies. The point is that they derive their direction and style from a first generation of professional managers. These people are building images of quality and professionalism about their businesses, entrusting to the outside world a continuing set of corporate values whose stability is not dependent on family succession.

2. Autonomy

Plainly, the capacity for delegation provides the crucial link between leadership and executive action. The efficient management of large, multi-product businesses may have to be predicated on rigorous decentralization policies such as those employed by Racal; for smaller companies this is not a common problem: their modest size enables them to enjoy the benefits of avoiding long channels of communication, diffusion of corporate purpose and unnecessary intra-organization rivalries.

Nevertheless, the action of devolving responsibilities down the line to smaller, discrete operating units is observable in some smaller companies. A notable example is Brengreen Holdings' approach to running commercial and industrial cleaning contracts, worth just over £30 million in 1983. David Evans is a staunch advocate of deep-rooted decentralization, for one overwhelming reason – the need to provide unfailingly good service to customers. He sees this objective as the linchpin of the business and therefore insists that no contracts manager, however ambitious and talented, takes on sufficient work to jeopardize client confidence that the job will be done and done well. The acid test of David Evans' commitment to this ideal was to push his own company and his competitors to a position where commercial cleaning contracts became renewable on a month by month basis. The confidence, some might say arrogance, with which Evans relies upon Brengreen's ability to retain customer loyalty – even in the face of price-cutting cowboys endemic in the industry – is ample testimony to his powers of delegating responsibility for service quality and profitability.

In general, however, the 'To centralize . . . or not?' question does not appear to rank as a great issue for our smaller companies. Where it matters, central control is tightly exercised – Iceland behaves much as Bejam or Sainsbury in clearly circumscribing the discretion available to store managers – where it does not, generous helpings of discretion are dispensed by senior managers predisposed to await the benefits of such risk-taking rather than to worry about the down-side or, even worse, to rely on elegant but stifling bureaucracies.

David Gration's biotech company, Boots-Celltech, neatly illustrates the importance of sowing the autonomy seed early in the life of a business aspiring to the heights of our winners. If his company is to gain the stature of the Racals of this world, he must solve two vital problems. First, as a general manager born out of the marketing function, how is he to direct a team of highly skilled but specialized biotechnologists whose understanding of commercial realities bears no better microscopic examination than does his of the bio-science of his research director? And, second, how will he cope with the prospect of the 30 per cent-plus compound growth rates commonplace among our smaller and larger winners? The solution to both these problems lies in the ability to select the right talent, to train it intelligently, and then to develop it by conferring the opportunities for this to happen. All of these stages require imagination, courage and backing to be overtly exercised by those at the top.

Gent's Production Director, Colin Craker, tells the story of how he selected a production director for one of the company's overseas subsidiaries. He had once been faced with the problem of how to sew mechanically the multitude of pleats required for a new design of skirt. Fashions change rapidly, so he had to move quickly. The laborious task of developing a new machine – well within the technical capability of his own people – was just not on. So he made several trips at home and abroad, scouring his own and other industries for ideas. As we shall see later, this instinct is endemic in Gent. Eventually, by accident, he happened on a curtain manufacturer who had of course long since solved this problem. Drawing on this experience, he posed the same problem to the contenders for the new job, asking 'What would *you* do?' The purpose? To isolate the candidate who appreciated the fast-moving nature of the business and could resist the temptation for conventional solutions only.

At Iceland Frozen Foods, Malcolm Walker and Peter Hinchcliffe are always striving for growth coupled with improved efficiency. In-store training was one problem that grabbed their attention. Experience had taught them that so many retailers who set aside normal opening hours for this purpose simply wasted the opportunity – it was just an excuse for time off. It was not to be so at Iceland. Their growth had taken them to the point of needing a full-time professional trainer, so they poached the best they could find – from Marks & Spencer! This strategy carried its own risks. On the plus side, it was plain that the new recruit was sufficiently well motivated by Iceland's prospects to forsake the prosperity and security all but guaranteed by her ex-employer. On the downside, might she not be frustrated by Iceland's smallness – after all, its turnover was under £10 million against M&S's fast-approaching £2 billion – and would she get the resources she was accustomed to? Walker and Hinchcliffe responded with the provision of two graduate assistants and a no-expense-spared video-making facility, with video players and monitors in every store. The result?

A series of highly professional and engaging videos covering all aspects of efficient store management designed to use, not waste, the time available.

Sodastream is an object lesson in embracing sophisticated manufacturing technology – and that, by a company and chief executive best known for their marketing flair. Up to a few years ago, Sodastream had virtually no manufacturing capability. Gas cylinders and flavour concentrates came from major suppliers such as BOC and Britvic. As Stephen Bingham freely admits, Sodastream did not rank greatly in their scheme of things. His company merely assembled bought-out components into the now familiar dispensers and refilled empty gas bottles as these were returned from retail outlets. How was he to get the supply side flexibility and cost structure the company so desperately needed? Knowing nothing of gas cylinder production technology himself, he hired the brightest graduate engineers he could find and set them to design, build and commission a complete manufacturing plant – from scratch! He was told he was a fool! Gas cylinder technology was complicated in itself, so much so that even the big companies could not apply the cost-effective extrusion methods used to make conventional large cylinders to the small ones which Sodastream required. Nothing daunted, Bingham entrusted the task of solving that problem to his young team. Less than ten years after it had no capability whatsoever, the company is now widely regarded as the international leader in small cylinder production technology.

One final example will highlight how senior management can, if it wishes, stimulate even quite junior employees to welcome both substantial responsibilities and the risks which go with them. At Gent, Peter Wolff explains how the company's present-day fortunes have their origin in a decision to push design for fashion amongst women's clothing retailed by Marks & Spencer. Today, the commitment to that decision has resulted in the company employing a design team of over eighty people producing more than 250 original or variation designs per week. Most of the designers are young women recently recruited from design college. Their task is to interpret fashions in colours, shapes, textures and so on in order that the company can offer a large choice of new and exciting styles to M&S buyers. When this writer visited the company in 1983, as a prelude to its eventual winning of the Business Enterprise Award, one stop was the design office. Peter Wolff was explaining the task of putting together the week's batch of new designs when, without warning, he turned to a young woman who was inspecting one of the new designs with a couple of her colleagues. 'What have you been doing lately?' he asked. Bold as brass came the reply 'Oh, I've just got back from a Paris exhibition and another in . . .'. It transpired she had used her own initiative along with the company's time and money to pick up yet another new idea. Mind you, a few yards further on, he made an impatient grab for a new blue dressing-gown, hauling it off the hanger, exclaiming 'That's awful! Its boring!' Within a few seconds, the rewards and risks of aggressive but imaginative delegation had been dramatically revealed.

3. Control

In December 1982 Iceland's Malcom Walker and Peter Hinchcliffe saw the opportunity of acquiring the eighteen-store St Catherine's frozen food chain based in the south-west. If successful, this would enhance the company's geographic representation greatly. But the asking price was £1.7 million, and Bejam were in the wings. Indeed, since some of the stores were located practically next door to Bejam, the takeover presaged the first head-on collision between two ambitious rivals who had thus far contained their coverage to separate halves of the country. A deal was struck in February 1983, by which time Iceland's men reckoned the victim had two weeks to live: huge loss-making was rampant, so much so that the agreed price had fallen below £600,000. Had they bought a pup? Or could they turn it round quickly enough to avoid disaster and then make money? Within three weeks the victim's head office and depot were closed and Iceland's customary yardsticks of performance and control vigorously applied. The St Catherine's operation survived, saved two hundred jobs and became profitable by the spring of the same year.

Here was an object lesson in applying the standards of a winner to a one-time loser. Certainly, the early focus of attention was on financial control: it had to be. But the key to unlocking the potential of the new company was to know where to look for weaknesses before taking corrective action. Walker and Hinchcliffe knew full well what kind of cost structure and sales productivity standards, particularly, should apply to an efficient frozen food chain. They had learned, sometimes the hard way, to distinguish between that which was crucial and that which was not. In this sense, the control practices of our smaller companies match very closely those of the larger winners.

Sadly, however, it seems that the financial lobby in many companies can become a 'dead hand', crushing the spirit of entrepreneurship and commercial adventure. More than one study of business planning in the UK has revealed the overwhelming supremacy of financial planning even where comparatively little is known about corporate intentions for marketing, organization development and so on. The single, most telling criticism which can be levelled at the door of budgetary control techniques is that they can constrain managers' perceptions of what may be possible for the sake of myopic satisfaction in meeting short-term targets. There is little evidence of this proclivity in our smaller winners. Flexibility is their by-word. Priorities are vigorously encouraged to adapt to changing commercial conditions. Nowhere is this attitude more striking than in market planning, product design and quality control.

Gent provides a good illustration of planning for the speculative opportunities conferred by uncertainty. Peter Wolff disarmingly defers to the judgement of his financial director, Bernard Adler, when setting the size of his fabric-buying 'slush fund'. This 'appropriation' derives from the quite explicit acknowledgement that the company is in the fashion business and that the 'personality' of a fabric may be crucial to the popularity of whichever garments incorporate it.

Consequently, Wolff equips himself each year with a cash quota to buy significant quantities, if not the entire supply, of new materials which just might catch
on in a big way. There is no guarantee that they will, but in the jargon of the
economist, the opportunity cost of failing to take the gamble may be gigantic.
Conveniently for some, the profit and loss account merely shows what was, not
what might have been!

That said, tight financial control is widely regarded as a prerequisite for
success. Many companies appear to treat it almost as a test of corporate virility
that weekly trading accounts are made available to top management by the
following Monday. At Iceland their one-time auditor, now finance director,
Bernard Leigh, is renowned for his computer-based management information
system, including weekly detailed profit and loss accounts for every one of their
stores and for the company in total.

Poaching financial specialists from obvious and not so obvious sources of
talent is commonplace. Consultants are particularly vulnerable; one company
hired a financial planner from a leading financial modelling software house
once they had seen him in action on their premises; Sodastream relieved Coop-
ers & Lybrand of one of its management consultants, who became financial
director; whilst Gent looked to BL's Innocenti operation in Italy for their man,
Bernard Adler. As with their counterparts in larger companies, these men (alas,
no women!) regard speed as of the essence in financial control, and they infuse
their colleagues with the same outlook. Our smaller winners are all committed to
securing information to plan and control their presence in the marketplace and
their standing against competitors. Iceland habitually uses market research data
whose quantity and quality would put many a larger retailer to shame. Without
doubt, this enables them to direct their store development programme with great
precision, but Walker and Hinchcliffe do not deceive themselves into thinking
that anything other than results matter in the end. Sales per employee is a
crucial measure of efficiency in retailing. When I visited the company for the
1983 Business Enterprise Award, I asked 'What do you achieve and how do you
compare with Bejam?' The answer to the first question was instantaneous – the
current year's projection was £75,000. The second part took a little
longer, but within the hour their in-house art department had produced a
coloured graphic showing that they were just on the point of overtaking Bejam,
whilst leaving M&S, Sainsbury and Tesco well behind. Here was ample
evidence of the speed with which the company could respond to key questions
about its competitiveness.

The importance of feedback does not stop there. The nature of Iceland's business – the retailing of perishable foodstuffs – means that stock control and
customer servicing levels are crucial to its fortunes. A few years ago the company
became acutely aware that its single, quarter of a million cubic-feet cold store
was in danger of bursting at the seams unless deliveries in and out were well
matched. The problem was to relay as rapidly as possible the re-order requirements of each of their stores, to get them 'picked' and delivered in double-quick

time whilst keeping close track of stock levels and replenishment needs at the central cold store.

In a manner typical of all of our highly successful smaller companies, Iceland looked to the practice of other large and successful food retailers. It soon became apparent that some form of electronic information technology was required. Store managers needed a quick and easy way to assemble and collate re-order data from visual inspection of stock levels in their freezer units and to transmit these data to the company's head office on the Deeside Industrial Park. Even the most advanced systems they could find in the UK did not satisfy them, and so they jumped on a plane to the United States to see what Safeway and others were doing.

Eventually they found what they wanted – a system which equipped each store manager with a walkie-talkie type handset into which all of the necessary information could be punched as he toured his store. Each handset had a detachable memory module which could be plugged into a special telephone socket in the manager's office. Each day at a duly appointed time, in a prearranged sequence, the head office computer would automatically dial up each store, retrieve the new information and immediately set about scheduling the next set of deliveries, recalculating stock positions and advising forward-buying requirements. The system was fiendishly expensive, but Walker and Hinchcliffe were determined to have the best technology available and anyway, the cost would be trivial if they used their new information to full advantage.

Iceland's approach is only one example of an obsessive instinct amongst our companies to discover and react to the changing mood of the marketplace with speed that would daunt the bulk of UK companies. But perhaps the most dramatic illustration of this phenomenon can be found at Gent. After Peter Wolff and his colleagues have transported their new batch of designs to M&S each Wednesday night and reviewed them with the buyers the following day, their attention turns to the new lines which are just hitting the racks of M&S's Baker Street and other big stores. Wolff and his colleagues are renowned for assailing M&S customers of a Saturday morning in order to gauge consumer reactions. 'What made you come back to this dress, after looking at those other two?' and other questions in similar vein. Sometimes the reactions are not all that might be expected! Nevertheless, Wolff says they can gauge market sentiment for some lines within ten or fifteen minutes of their appearance on the hangers. By Saturday evening he can telephone their headquarters in Barnsley saying in so many words, 'Drop whatever you can and push *these* lines for all you can get' or 'Stop this blouse or that skirt *now*'. Production in the factories can respond almost instantaneously as computer-controlled cutting machines are reprogrammed at the push of a button and no demarcation issues exist to stifle flexibility.

Control, then, is regarded as a powerful instrument of management whose areas of application are selected with great care before it is vigorously exercised. The dead hand of elaborate bureaucracies and wilfully punitive control systems is avoided like the plague, for they are seen as stupidly counter-productive and anathema to a corporate culture whose ethos is to enjoy the winning but not at *any* price.

4. Involvement

Just as with our large companies, each of the smaller success stories is imbued with a measure of energy, commitment and involvement from chief executive to bottle washer, quite uncharacteristic of so many business concerns.

The episode just described at Gent took place at six-thirty p.m. one Wednesday evening. Clock-watching there was anathema – the new delivery had to be got on the road that night and everyone knew, without being told, that they would be there till it was done. Ceremony, toes and rules would be ruthlessly trampled on by anyone and everyone to achieve the common goal – and that was not to get home as soon as possible!

In a more relaxed vein, Gent make extensive use of two notable mechanisms for fostering employee involvement – quality circles and job rotation. Several quality circles exist, though they come and go as problems arise and are solved; they are not allowed to become institutionalized talking-shops. Job rotation is actively encouraged and, within reason, almost anything goes. There is nothing beyond aptitude and motivation to prevent a seamstress from switching to console operator of a sophisticated computer-aided design and manufacturing system developed out of the aerospace industry. Amongst other benefits, this policy discourages job demarcation, endemic in the textiles industry.

Stories of crisis resolution abound in our smaller companies as they do in the larger ones, and little extra can be learned from their experiences: except, one is tempted to say, that young habits tend to grow into older ones.

Similarly, the success of our small- to medium-sized companies is closely correlated with a desire and the ability to pay above-average wages and benefits. Indeed, it is interesting to observe how sensitive these companies can be to the subtleties of labour markets, even though they do not abound with welfare or any other brand of economists!

Brengreen offers a dramatic illustration of the results which can be obtained from people once they become actively involved in the business and are strongly motivated to contribute to its success. The company really began to take off when, in 1980, it won the first local authority cleaning contract in the initiative to privatize public sector services. David Evans admits that luck was on his side. His company beat Pritchard by £21,000 on a £1.762 million contract, which was destined to save Southend ratepayers some £600,000 a year. All 250 refuse collectors and other employees were offered jobs with Brengreen. Early retirement, natural wastage and – as Evans describes them –

discredited trade unionists resulted in 190 being taken on. For these, David Evans was able to offer the prospect of 30 per cent wages enhancement and the first £10,000-a-year dustmen in the country – provided they worked a genuine eight-hour day rather than the four-hour day allowed by the previous regime. Smart uniforms and new and efficient vehicles (leased for two years maximum to ensure modernity) were two further contributors to improved productivity, as was a new business incentive scheme designed to encourage refuse collectors themselves to generate new trade.

Notwithstanding their similar approach to high pay, smaller companies seem much less disposed toward profit-sharing schemes than their larger counterparts. This propensity may come as a disappointment to those whose political ideology incorporates this form of employee participation. But the reasons advanced are compelling. First, it is said, these companies are in the formative stages of their development and this means they are committed to unprecedented levels of capital expenditure designed to secure long-run prosperity. The inevitable consequence is artificial pressure upon profits, and also therefore the capacity to share in them! A high-wage policy provides a simple and equitable solution to the temporal limitations of accounting. Second, what is to happen if profits take a tumble or, even worse, losses are incurred? Better a policy based upon demonstrable ability to pay than one geared to a profits record whose future trend is neither inexorable nor guaranteed. The experience of Gent provides useful testimony to the virtue of this kind of philosophy, disagreeably paternalistic though it may be to some.

A few years ago Marks & Spencer experienced a period during which it became severely uncompetitive – on price. The company insisted that its suppliers shoulder a 5 per cent price cut. Despite its symbiotic relationship with M&S, Gent was not immune and their burgeoning profits growth was noticeably dented. This was scarcely the fault of their employees, and yet a profit-sharing scheme would have made it appear so to all intents and purposes. The *quid pro quo* arose when the company went public on an offer for sale by tender in mid-1983. Wolff and Wetzel saw this event as the right opportunity to reward their workers for their past efforts and to give them a stake in the company's future prosperity. Even though it was to be at the expense of their personal wealth, the two men argued that their employees should be entitled to subscribe for shares at the minimum tender price of 160p, even though everyone expected this to be much lower than the striking price. This was all but heresy to the self-regulatory instincts of the City and Gent's advisers argued accordingly. Nevertheless, the joint owners were adamant and, flying in the face of their advisers, they took their cause to the Stock Exchange itself. It seems that the sheer temerity with which they took on the City fathers made such an impression as to force an historic concession. The share issue was a great success, with the striking price being set at 190p and opening dealings at 200p.

5. Market orientation

It will be apparent by now that the perceived importance of attending to the marketplace is bound up, integrally, with many if not all of our other ingredients for success. Indeed, that fact tempts one to speculate on whether marketing is not after all the linchpin of business enterprise. Of course, a multitude of arguments abound to ascribe the supreme business objective to people, profits, products or any other fundamental which takes the fancy of the particular protagonist. On close examination most and probably all of these propositions default on grounds of circular and/or contingent logic. Yet all of our small winners, and most of our larger ones, do seem to give quite exceptional attention – in terms of skills, time and money – to getting the right product in the right place at the right time for the right price. There is no earth-shattering revelation here; not even, one suspects, for those companies and chief executives who still persist in relying on the market to come to them rather than the other way around!

Of the factors which went to make up the market orientation in our sample of large companies, the least contiguous here is maintenance of brand strength. Where applicable, the emphasis is more upon the creation of a brand image as in the case of Sodastream. Stephen Bingham was faced with a fascinating dilemma over his fizzy drinks system. A brand name existed, albeit buried in the annals of history, but it had no obvious market orientation. Did it belong with consumer durables, like food mixers, to be bought in electrical retailers, or did it belong among the food and soft drink counters of, say, Sainsbury? This problem took some thinking through before he decided they were in fizzy drinks first and appliances second. With that matter resolved, Sodastream could then devote its substantial advertising budget to promoting a well-defined brand image via its now famous television commercials.

A notable example is Coloroll. This company was for many years a sleepy, privately owned business based in Lancashire, making paper and plastic carrier bags. Eventually the company was to feel the draught of a new chief executive who saw the potential for the company in the entirely new field of wallpaper. The market was declining in the wake of cheaper and easier emulsion paint; moreover it was dominated by the few 'sleeping giants' of the industry.

Coloroll gained its second place in the wall coverings market by the judicious mixture of several interlocking devices. The real breakthrough came with the introduction of Linda Beard's new and refreshing 'Dolly Mixture' range of patterns designed to catch the spirit of the time. These were to be followed by a series of designs for children's rooms incorporating popular television cartoon characters. Copyright deals would quickly be done with the likes of Walt Disney: its Superman pattern comprehensively broke all industry records for a new launch.

Coloroll's stock availability had to be exceptional. Accordingly a small tele-sales team was set up in their converted cotton-mill headquarters in Nelson, Lancashire. Its task was to check every UK retailer's stock position every ten days. In this way prospective retailers could be convinced that higher stock turn would yield higher profits than other suppliers could offer – even to the point where Coloroll's products were to be found on the empty display racks of their competitors!

Iceland had a rather different experience with aggressive sales promotion. In order to get one of their new freezer centres off to a good start, they hired Terry Wogan to make the opening. Publicity was organized and so effective was it that the store was inundated with Wogan admirers – in fact, so many that no one could move to get their hands on the frozen peas and Black Forest gateaux! Reluctantly, that ploy could not be repeated and the company took solace in more conventional methods of promotion and advertising.

Quality assurance is as vital for frozen foods as other products. Even for a modestly sized company such as theirs, Malcolm Walker and Peter Hinchcliffe insisted on employing a well-qualified home economist with a fully equipped kitchen in their head office. Her task was and is to test all of the company's products, branded and own-label, on whomever she can find to eat them. Just as in Sainsbury, the directors are avid tasters. Lots of time is spent out and about at Women's Institutes and similar organizations, giving demonstrations of how to store and use the various meats, vegetables, sweets and other products.

As one would expect, Gent is intimately concerned with Marks & Spencer's renowned policy for quality control. The company is regularly visited by M&S representatives keen to ensure the highest possible quality. This manifestation of the two companies' close relationship is judged to be a real virtue, not an irritant. But the relationship cuts both ways. Much of Gent's spectacular success undoubtedly comes from its ability to persuade M&S to stock fashionable goods – clothes to be bought on impulse rather than for reasons of utility and longevity. In this sense, the company can be viewed as a beneficent thorn in the side of its customer, provoking it into new business which might not otherwise be countenanced. A lesson for suppliers in general?

Brengreen's Evans makes a point of telling you his company was the first to make use of an appealing sales brochure in the industrial and commercial cleaning market. It shows off their flagship contracts such as the Houses of Parliament and the Stock Exchange.

So, all of these companies see the marketplace as the source of their life blood. But they don't just talk about it, they apply themselves with such energy and conviction that they can scarcely fail to win.

6. Zero basing

Sticking to the last is rather like using a double-edged cut-throat razor – by all means keep the chin trim but take care not to slit the jugular! Thus far none of our smaller winners have been seriously tempted to do someone else's thing.

Coloroll did make an imaginative – some might say hazardous – jump into textile co-ordinates on the back of their success in wall coverings. But they took great care not to delude themselves about their strengths and weaknesses. The former included innovative design skills, proven printing abilities and a rare flair for marketing; the latter certainly included no experience of textiles manufacture. Consequently, the company struck a deal with Vantona at a time when that company was hard-pressed for business and therefore keen to supply to quality and price specifications attractive to Coloroll. The company was thus able to piggy-back bedspreads, curtains and similar soft furnishings on to their wall coverings operation, whilst avoiding the risks of getting into a business which they did not understand.

Companies such as Sodastream, Brengreen, Iceland and Gent have undoubtedly found their success in doing well that which they know, in buoyant markets largely of their own making. The interesting conundrum is to know what they will do if and when their markets run out of steam or their growth aspirations outpace the potential of their existing lines of business. Will they succumb to the temptation to dabble in other areas, even to play that so seductive game of takeovers? One suspects not. They all appear to know their limitations, whilst being sufficiently confident in their ability to innovate that the foreseeable future contains no spectre of corporate decay. Time will tell.

7. Innovation

Innovation is endemic in these companies' life systems, whether in products, people or processes. It is quintessentially attitudinal in nature and not the predictable residue of some curious alchemy. Nonetheless, as in the nurture of a species of delicate flower, there do appear to be certain conditions which are conducive to its furtherance. These are basically the same in small firms as in large ones, although the emphasis on each varies somewhat.

Barriers to change are hard to find amongst the likes of Gent, Sodastream and the other star performers. The reasons for this are difficult to pinpoint, but they do seem to include the following:

- prevention of unnecessary power bases, bureaucracies and vested interests
- iconoclastic attitudes amongst managers *and* subordinates
- keen awareness of the penalties suffered by unbending competitors
- clear exposition by top management of the potential benefits of change before *and* after its implementation
- explicit personal incentive (money, promotion, and so on) to risk change

Each of these ingredients was at one time or another central to the various innovations recounted already.

The capacity for curiosity in one's own and other industries at home and abroad has, we hope, been amply illustrated by the technology experiences of S.R. Gent and Iceland Frozen Foods. But consider one more case. Imagine yourself in

Stephen Bingham's shoes running Sodastream, and ask yourself 'What chance that no product like ours exists in the US market, with its gargantuan appetite for Coca-Cola and the like?'. If, as Bingham did, you took the question seriously and went there to find out, the answer would have been 100 per cent. An unlikely tale, but a true one.

One final story goes a long way to capturing the essence of innovation in our smaller winners.

By late 1980 Iceland Frozen Foods was on the point of outgrowing its quarter of a million cubic-feet cold store at its headquarters in Clwyd. Turnover was then under £9 million, but their intended growth rate visualized £14 million in 1981, £24 million in 1982 and, as it was to transpire, £46 million in 1983. Their original cold store had only been built in 1979, when they became the first tenant on the ex-BSC Shotton site, but it was already bursting at the seams. An extra one had to be built which, together with a new administration block, was going to consume almost £2 million when their net assets were only £800,000. But Malcolm Walker and Peter Hinchcliffe had the courage of their convictions – they would build the most advanced cold store ever, sufficient in size to quintuple their storage capacity at one fell swoop. They scoured the world for the most advanced but proven technology they could find; from compressor units and insulation material to integrated palletization between the cold store and their refrigerated trucks. Not content with current racking technology they designed, installed and buried for future excavation a complete set of tracks to anticipate automated 'picking'. Meanwhile, attention was paid to the sub-zero working conditions of their forklift truck drivers. At a trade exhibition they found one truck manufacturer who, as an experiment, had built a prototype with insulated cab, heating and even a stereo system! To their surprise, Iceland ordered three despite their high cost. As of late 1983, they were the only ones ever built.

Innovation did not stop at technology. Subsidized loan finance was obtained via the European Coal and Steel Community, and the British Rail Pension Fund subscribed additional preference share capital. The relationship with the latter was in itself imaginative, for it enabled Iceland to gain 'anchor tenant' status as it sought additional outlets in new high street shopping developments – a privilege normally confined to publicly listed companies judged worthy of participation by the large investing institutions.

This innovation and risk-taking paid off handsomely. Growth accelerated at an electrifying rate, their unexpected acquisition was readily assimilated and their cold store became the flagship location for many of their equipment suppliers. Walker and Hinchcliffe take justifiable pride in showing off their technological masterpiece to whoever is interested – except, of course, the competition!

8. Integrity

'Of course it's vital .... Next question!' would be the response we could expect from all our smaller winners.

Conclusion

What conclusions can we draw from this? In most important respects the eight perceptions of our large winners are also present in the smaller fry. Differences of emphasis do exist, as one would expect. They appear to stem from two principal sources.

First, many large companies obtain their size by basing growth on a wide range of activities, often diverse in nature. This approach calls for special managerial talents to handle problems of decentralization and complex, sometimes diffuse corporate cultures. Smaller, simpler companies do not have to contend with these issues as a rule.

Second, the leaders of very large businesses are obliged to take special cognizance of their economic, social and sometimes political prominence. Policies governing corporate integrity and employee involvement, especially, will often be the object of intense public scrutiny. Smaller companies take the substance of these issues equally seriously but with less regard for image management.

Incidentally, none of our smaller winners are run by beady-eyed autocrats. The marketing fraternity appears to have the upper hand. As for MBAs, there are none amongst our small population, but you could look to Henley graduate Larry Tracey, who became a millionaire when recently floating his company, Powerline, on the Unlisted Securities Market!

Peter J. A. Herbert is a member of the Directing Staff at Henley – The Management College. The views expressed here are those of the author and not the College.

Appendix 2 Three statements of company philosophy

From STC's 'Best Company Book'

Overall Objectives

Products and Customers
To provide quality, reliability and good value in the products and services we sell.

To be sensitive and responsive to changing customer needs from product development to after-sales service.

To develop the right relationships between the Company and all its customers. To maintain proper communication and co-operation between sales organizations so that the customers' needs are met simply and effectively.

Profit
To achieve high and increasing levels of profit, so enabling us to meet our responsibilities to shareholders, employees, customers and suppliers, and to the community as a whole.

To improve our competitiveness by constantly enhancing the performance of our manufacturing, engineering, installation, marketing and administrative functions.

Innovation
To encourage ideas for new and improved products, for new applications of technology and for improvements in manufacturing skills and efficiency.

To give full consideration to the problems and opportunities before entering new fields, while accepting that properly quantified risks must sometimes be taken.

People
To enable people to share in the Company's success; to recognize their individual achievements; to help them attain satisfaction and a sense of accomplishment from their work; to seek to provide job security.

To foster a spirit of co-operation between individuals and groups, and trust and understanding between managers and their people, based on the belief of

182

employees in the good faith and integrity of their colleagues, managers and the Company as a whole.

To provide opportunities for advancement based upon individual initiative, ability and accomplishment, and to give employees appropriate opportunities to improve their skills and capabilities and prepare themselves for more responsible jobs.

Management
To provide objectives and leadership which generate enthusiasm at all levels; to select managers who are not only enthusiastic themselves but who have the ability to engender enthusiasm among their colleagues.

To practise management to the highest standards of competence and to employ the best available techniques; to ensure that the leadership exercised by each manager, at whatever level, should have balanced regard for the task, the team and the individual.

To ensure that those Company-wide policies whose observance is mandatory are clearly defined, are made known to employees and are kept up to date.

To encourage intiative, enterprise and creativity; to emphasize what is to be done while leaving room whenever possible for creative solutions compatible with the overall goal.

Relations with the Community
To be an economic, intellectual and social asset to the local community, the nation, the EEC, and the world as a whole.

To respect the environment and to be sensitive to the interests of people living in the neighbourhoods in which we have plants.

To encourage people to fulfil their personal sense of duty to the community as well as their objectives within the Company.

To help in finding the solutions to national problems by contributing knowledge and talent.

To conduct the Company's affairs with honesty and integrity. People at every level will be expected to adhere to high standards of business ethics, and the Company will comply with the spirit as well as the letter of the law.

To pursue a policy of equality of opportunity whereby all personnel actions will be administered regardless of race, colour, religion or sex.

Style
To be concerned with performance and results and ensure that the method of achievement of short-term targets does not jeopardize long-range growth. The climate in which these objectives shall be pursued will be open and communicative and encourage the exercise of initiative, enterprise and creativity. Employees should enjoy satisfaction and a sense of accomplishment from their involvement and participation in the work.

To attempt to combine the accountability, flexibility and freedom characteristic of a small company with the strengths of a large organization.

To harness the combined efforts of each individual in the organization towards common goals by providing objectives which are realistic and clearly understood by everyone and which reflect the basic character and personality of the organization.

Standards

To adopt the best standards of corporate and individual behaviour. On corporate standards this means, for example, making fair contracts, ensuring equal opportunity. On individual behaviour, it means for example that no manager will offer or accept a financial inducement such as to be likely to corrupt. It also implies that whatever is attempted by the Company or its managers will be to the best possible standard of achievement, while also being sensible, practical and economical.

H.P. Bulmer Holdings Limited

Statement of Company Objectives

We believe that success in any company can be achieved only if every employee understands and supports the objectives which the company, and each individual in it, is striving to attain. Each year we review and, after consultation with the Employee Council, where necessary revise them. The wording amended this year is printed in italics.

These objectives are not necessarily all of equal importance and at different times some may require more attention than others.

1. To increase profitability and earnings per share each year by improving our added value (the amount which remains after the cost of materials and bought-in services has been deducted from sales income) not only as a proportion of sales income but also in terms of the average amount generated by each employee.

2. To give the utmost consideration to the needs and interests of our customers, and to retain our leading position in the cider and pectin markets.

3. To pay the best wage and salary rates we can afford, and to ensure job satisfaction for all employees through enlightened management. To improve working conditions wherever possible and take all appropriate steps to ensure the health and safety of all employees. To promote the best possible human relations and a situation in which people really enjoy working for the company.

4. To remain an independent public company with a distinctive management style.

5. To give executives the maximum freedom of action, and to encourage them to make the fullest use of it, so that they can personally influence profits.

6. To continue to encourage employee participation in the ownership of the company. The group profit-sharing scheme is an important step in achieving this objective.

7. To keep employees informed of policy, progress and problems, to invite comments and criticisms and to show everyone how individual effort contributes to the company's success.

8. To be flexible and not to depend too much on any one product, customer or market. To maximize the advantage which is to be obtained from the recent extension of our range of products and to continue to broaden the base of the trading activities of the group at home and overseas. To maintain an efficient research and development policy so that opportunities can be quickly recognized and speedily exploited.

9. To avoid redundancy *and promote job security* by careful forward planning and by the early recognition of the effects of change.

10. To train and develop all employees and to promote from within whenever possible. When a position must be filled from outside, to recruit the best possible person available.

11. To ensure the future supply of our vital raw materials.

12. To benefit the local community whenever and wherever the group can afford to do so, and to preserve the quality of life and of the environment.

Saatchi & Saatchi

Outlook for the Company

In analysing the Company's prospects in the 1980s we think it is important for us to adopt the same disciplines as we recommend to our clients for their brands – *to be sharp in the definition of our long-term objectives, frank about our genuine strengths and weaknesses, and clear about our position in the market.*

What are our Basic Strengths?
1. Our People
We believe that we have a management and staff with a striking record of success – achieved at a young enough age to still retain momentum and drive for the future. Our management team knows that our business cannot be dependent on a few key people – at all levels and in all departments we feel we are staffed by exceptional men and women.

How have we achieved this? Because we have had *the financial strength and stability to pay the best rates, the creative and marketing standards to attract the best people, and the growth prospects to keep them.*

As well as this, the Company team has a tremendous additional stake in the business – the Company's management is also the Company's largest shareholder.

2. Our Clients

We are fortunate to work with a number of great companies. Many of them are the leaders in their field, and with most of them we have enjoyed a good relationship for many years.

Much of our strength as a company today stems from the benefit of this working experience with some of the world's most professional consumer-goods manufacturers.

3. Our Organization

Our organizational structure has the great advantage of being *simple*. The Company is divided into autonomous business units responsible to a parent Company, which sets basic financial policies – annual goals of performance, reporting procedures etc.

Hopefully, this set-up means that the key men in the operating companies are not bankers, lawyers or accountants, but advertising professionals.

The parent Company agrees objectives with them, creates clear lines of responsibility for achieving these objectives, provides the authority to do so, applies standard measurement techniques so that everyone is operating on the same known ground-rules and ensures rewards for success.

This simple structure means that we are well placed to seize any opportunities which may arise, and to weather any problems which will arise – at least as well, and frankly we believe better, than most.

We are sometimes asked whether the fact that the Company is listed on the Stock Exchange makes a difference to the way we run our advertising agency business. The answer is – hardly at all. As a quoted Company we run our business as any business should be – in business-like fashion. We do this with a system of management controls not dissimilar to those used in any reasonably large company. We write a plan, we monitor achievement against that plan and we try to signal trouble ahead – with a large flag!

4. The International Network

Our association with the Compton International network gives us the benefit of a formal relationship with one of the strongest agency networks, with offices in most major marketing centres of the world.

5. Style and Approach

We believe much of the real, long-term success of any company is attributable not so much to its products at any point in time, or even to its people at any point, but rather to *its basic approach to the business* – its key policies, its guiding principles – in short, *its way of looking at things*.

We thought it would be worthwhile to spell out to you the guiding principles which have inspired our own progress over the years:

Our Approach to Advertising
a) We believe that *one of our 30-second commercials for a product should be worth 60 seconds of advertising from its competitor*. To achieve this, the Agency does not adopt any creative 'house style' or 'tone of voice'. We believe that a hard sell is right for some situations, mood and imagery for others, and humour for others. Our advertising has only one linking factor – *it tries to make a single minded proposition 'come alive' in a compelling way*.
b) We want to grow – but *most of all we want to grow with our existing clients*. The new business won from an existing client is doubly rewarding – it means not only the increase in billings that comes with any new account, but also that you have strengthened a working relationship. (And, of course, a track record of gaining more and more business from one's existing clients is in itself reassuring and attractive to potential new clients.) In every way, this seems to us the most desirable form of new business and we try to set the standard of service on an account with this in mind.
c) We have always tried to be consistent and single minded about the type of agency we wanted to build. We have never been believers in small agencies which are dependent on the style of one or two top men, however outstanding those individuals may be. On the other hand we have had no desire to create a giant – if that meant operating along the lines of some grey nationalized industry. We have always aimed to create *the one type of agency which has somehow eluded the grasp of almost all those men and women who have tried to achieve it* – a *large* agency, certainly, with all the stability and security that gives to employees, and all the back-up that provides for clients – but one which *at the same time also succeeds in being progressive, youthful and innovative in approach*.

The fact that this combination has so rarely been achieved in our industry increases the sense of purpose with which we continue to pursue it as our goal.

Our Approach to Profitability
a) Any company's financial record is probably best measured against its basic financial objective. In our own case this means a *steady and consistent improvement in performance year by year*, and a growth pattern which avoids the thrills and spills sometimes associated with our industry.

We have always taken the view that the most solid 'asset' we can have is the management capacity to produce a steady growth in earnings – through thick and thin. Times like these, when the value of 'solid' assets like property or plant has recently proved so illusory, reinforce us in our aim to build and re-build this particular 'asset' every year.

b) We consider that growth can and should be 'managed' – and that, therefore, acquisitions can play a part in growth – provided they are made for sound commercial reasons and are in line with our general principles.

It is worth saying that in assessing any potential acquisition, our yardstick is not so much the effect it will have on our earnings, but rather on our earnings *per share* – we have no wish to 'build' the Company by diluting our most precious possession – the Company's equity.

What is our Overall Objective?

What is fundamental to all of these approaches is *a belief in excellence* – that in all spheres of life and at all times there will be a few performances which are excellent, a few which are very poor ... while the majority will be just average.

Our aim in all of our activities and at all times is *the avoidance of the average and the achievement of the excellent.* This applies to all aspects of the way we run our business – to the people we employ, to the advertising we run, to the way we buy our media, to the operating margins we expect.

All our standards are set by the 'norm' – whatever that is, by definition, there is a better way. This has been the fundamental spur to our growth over the years.

Appendix 3 The questionnaire

Many companies with high reputations were left out of our original survey, for a variety of reasons. Some were too small for meaningful comparisons; others, though profitable and currently admired by the stock market, had been through rough times which disqualified them from our success criteria; others were still in the grip of the recession. At our invitation the chairmen of fifteen of those companies ranked their companies against thirty-four characteristics of company style. These companies were:

Beecham Group
Blue Circle Industries
BP Co.
Cadbury Schweppes
Comet Group
Dalgety
Horizon Travel
Ladbroke Group
Laporte Industries (Holdings)
Northern Engineering Industries (NEI)
Rowntree Mackintosh
Sedgwick Group
Sirdar
Smiths Industries
Wm Morrison Supermarkets

Of these characteristics the first eight were the eight described by Peters and Waterman in *In Search of Excellence*. The rest were characteristics that surfaced in the discussions with our twenty-three very successful companies.

It is impossible to assess how objective the chairmen's answers were. Certainly, some were more modest than others and there was obvious reluctance to admit that their companies were poor in any of the characteristics. What is perhaps more significant is that these industrialists were willing to try to assess their organizations publicly in these terms. Also significant are those characteristics where few or none of them rated themselves as outstanding, particularly:

- a bias for action
- autonomy and entrepreneurship

- attention to employee communications
- a sense of ownership
- innovation
- clear and demanding objective setting
- clear corporate mission
- productivity orientation
- heavy emphasis on training
- above-average pay
- incentives.

This is, we suggest, an implicit recognition that much still remains to be done to change the culture of British industry.

The answers

Characteristics where companies consider themselves:
***   Outstanding
  **   Well above average
    *   Above average

US conclusions.

1 A bias for action
  **   Beecham
  **   Sirdar
  **   Sedgwick
  **   Blue Circle
  **   Laporte
  **   Ladbroke
  **   BP
    *   NEI
    *   Dalgety
    *   Comet
    *   Wm Morrison
    *   Horizon

2 Closeness to the customer
***   NEI
***   Sedgwick
***   Sirdar
***   Beecham
***   WM Morrison
***   Blue Circle
***   Rowntree Mackintosh
  **   Cadbury Schweppes
    *   Horizon

    *   Dalgety
    *   Laporte

3 Autonomy and entrepreneurship
***   Laporte
***   BP
  **   Comet
  **   Sedgwick
  **   Blue Circle
  **   Ladbroke
    *   Sirdar
    *   NEI
    *   Beecham
    *   Wm Morrison

4 Productivity through people
***   Comet Group
***   Blue Circle
  **   NEI
  **   Sirdar
  **   Wm Morrison
  **   Laporte
  **   Dalgety
    *   Horizon

* Ladbroke
* Smiths Inds.
* Beecham
* Cadbury Schweppes
* Sedgwick

5 Hands-on, value-driven
*** Wm Morrison
** Ladbroke
** Sirdar
** Rowntree Mackintosh
** NEI
** Smiths Inds.
** BP
** Dalgety
** Blue Circle
** Laporte
* Sedgwick
* Cadbury Schweppes
* Beecham

6 Sticking to the knitting
*** Sedgwick
*** Blue Circle
** Cadbury Schweppes
** Sirdar
** Ladbroke
** Rowntree Mackintosh
* Wm Morrison
* Smiths Inds.
* Horizon
* Dalgety
* Laporte

7 Simple form, lean staff
*** Wm Morrison
*** Beecham
*** Sirdar
*** Dalgety
** Horizon
** Laporte
* Ladbroke
* Smiths Inds.
* Blue Circle
* NEI
* Sedgwick

8 Simultaneous loose-tight properties
*** Sedgwick
*** Beecham
*** Laporte
*** Ladbroke
*** Dalgety
** NEI
** Wm Morrison
** Smiths Inds.
* BP
* Sirdar
* Cadbury Schweppes
* Blue Circle

Characteristics potentially common to UK companies.

9 Natural curiosity
** Wm Morrison
** Smiths Inds.
** Comet
** Sedgwick
** Sirdar
* Horizon
* Beecham
* Blue Circle
* NEI

10 International perspective
*** Beecham
*** Sedgwick
*** Laporte
*** BP
** Wm Morrison
** Ladbroke
** Smiths Inds.
** Comet
** Dalgety
** Blue Circle
** NEI
** Sirdar
* Horizon
* Cadbury Schweppes

11 Long term perspective
***   BP
***   Sedgwick
***   Comet
***   Wm Morrison
 **   Laporte
 **   Cadbury Schweppes
 **   Blue Circle
 **   Rowntree Mackintosh
  *   Sirdar
  *   NEI
  *   Beecham
  *   Smiths Inds.
  *   Ladbroke

12 Market orientation
***   Wm Morrison
***   Comet
***   Beecham
***   Rowntree Mackintosh
***   Cadbury Schweppes
***   Sedgwick
***   Sirdar
 **   Dalgety
 **   Blue Circle
 **   NEI
  *   Horizon
  *   Smiths Inds.

13 Attention to employee communications
 **   Cadbury Schweppes
 **   Smiths Inds.
 **   Wm Morrison
  *   Laporte
  *   Sirdar
  *   NEI
  *   Blue Circle
  *   Dalgety
  *   Rowntree Mackintosh
  *   Horizon

14 A Sense of Ownership
***   Horizon
 **   Wm Morrison
 **   Ladbroke
 **   Comet
 **   Laporte
  *   Smiths Inds.
  *   NEI
  *   Cadbury Schweppes
  *   Sirdar

15 Ability to get back to fundamentals
***   Dalgety
***   Wm Morrison
 **   BP
 **   Laporte
 **   NEI
 **   Rowntree Mackintosh
 **   Comet
 **   Ladbroke
  *   Sirdar
  *   Cadbury Schweppes
  *   Blue Circle
  *   Smiths Inds.
  *   Horizon

16 Innovation
***   Beecham
 **   Wm Morrison
 **   Ladbroke
 **   Smiths Inds.
 **   Dalgety
 **   Blue Circle
 **   Sedgwick
 **   Sirdar
  *   Horizon
  *   Laporte

17 The team concept
***   Ladbroke
***   Wm Morrison
 **   BP
 **   Sirdar
 **   NEI
 **   Sedgwick
 **   Dalgety
 **   Smiths Inds.

* Laporte
* Cadbury Schweppes
* Rowntree Mackintosh
* Comet

18 Clear leadership and direction
* * * Wm Morrison
* * * Ladbroke
* * * Beecham
* * * Dalgety
* * Smiths Inds.
* * Comet
* * Sedgwick
* * NEI
* * Sirdar
* * Laporte
* Horizon
* Blue Circle

19 Clear and demanding objective setting
* * * Ladbroke
* * Laporte
* * Sirdar
* * NEI
* * Sedgwick
* * Dalgety
* * Smiths Inds.
* * Wm Morrison
* Cadbury Schweppes
* Blue Circle
* Beecham
* Horizon

20 A clear corporate mission
* * * Laporte
* * Sedgwick
* Wm Morrison
* Smiths Inds.
* Beecham
* NEI
* Cadbury Schweppes
* Sirdar

21 Effective supplier relationships
* * * Sedgwick

* * * Wm Morrison
* * Sirdar
* * Rowntree Mackintosh
* Laporte
* Cadbury Schweppes
* NEI
* Blue Circle
* Dalgety
* Smiths Inds.
* Horizon

22 The right tools for the job
* * * Ladbroke
* * * Dalgety
* * * Sedgwick
* * Wm Morrison
* * Smiths Inds.
* * Sirdar
* * Laporte
* * BP
* NEI
* Cadbury Schweppes

23 Generalist rather than specialist managers
* * Smiths Inds.
* * Wm Morrison
* BP
* Laporte
* Sirdar
* NEI
* Sedgwick
* Comet

24 Attention to general corporate image
* * * Wm Morrison
* * * Sirdar
* * Smiths Inds.
* * Sedgwick
* * BP
* Horizon
* Ladbroke
* Blue Circle
* NEI

25 Information orientation
***   Smiths Inds.

**   Sirdar
**   Cadbury Schweppes
**   Rowntree Mackintosh
**   Ladbroke
**   Wm Morrison

*   NEI
*   Sedgwick
*   Blue Circle
*   Dalgety
*   Beecham

26 Productivity orientation
***   Sirdar

**   Horizon
**   Ladbroke
**   Smiths Inds.
**   Blue Circle
**   NEI
**   Cadbury Schweppes

*   Wm Morrison
*   Comet
*   Rowntree Mackintosh
*   Dalgety
*   Sedgwick
*   Laporte

27 Heavy emphasis on training
***   Ladbroke

**   Sirdar
**   Wm Morrison

*   Cadbury Schweppes
*   Sedgwick
*   Dalgety
*   Rowntree Mackintosh
*   Smiths Inds.
*   Horizon

28 Above average pay
**   Horizon
**   Beecham
**   Sedgwick
**   Sirdar

*   Ladbroke

*   Smiths Inds.
*   Cadbury Schweppes
*   NEI

29 Incentives
***   Laporte

**   Sirdar
**   Sedgwick

*   Cadbury Schweppes
*   Dalgety
*   Horizon
*   Comet

30 Promotion from within
***   Sedgwick
***   BP

**   Beecham
**   Comet
**   Rowntree Mackintosh
**   Wm Morrison
**   Blue Circle
**   Cadbury Schweppes
**   Sirdar

*   Dalgety
*   Ladbroke
*   Horizon
*   NEI
*   Laporte

31 Stimulating enjoyment of work
**   Sedgwick

*   Sirdar
*   Cadbury Schweppes
*   Dalgety
*   BP

32 Integrity
***   Wm Morrison
***   Sedgwick

**   BP
**   Smiths Inds.
**   Beechams
**   Comet
**   Rowntree Mackintosh

** Horizon
** NEI
** Cadbury Schweppes
** Sirdar
** Laporte
* Dalgety
* Ladbroke
* Blue Circle

33 Great attention to detail
*** Wm Morrison
** Sirdar
** Horizon
** Ladbroke
** Rowntree Mackintosh
** Comet
* Laporte
* Cadbury Schweppes
* Sedgwick
* Dalgety
* Smiths Inds.

34 Unswerving committment to growth
*** Beecham
*** Comet
*** Wm Morrison
*** Ladbroke
*** Sedgwick
*** NEI
** Smiths Inds.
** Dalgety
** Sirdar
* Horizon
* Laporte

35 Others:
People & job values
** Wm Morrison

Clarity in organization
*** Laporte

Diversification after expert management has been secured
*** Horizon

Bibliography

'Are Today's Managers Risk-shy?', *International Management*, May 1982.

John Argenti, *Corporate Collapse, the Causes and Symptoms*, McGraw-Hill, Maidenhead, 1976.

'Companies Show a New Gusto for Risk Taking', *International Management*, December 1983.

Kenneth Corfield, *Patterns of Change*, London, STC (published collection of speeches).

A.F.L. Deeson, *Great Company Crashes*, Foulsham, London, 1972.

Michael Edwardes, *Back from the Brink*, Collins, London, 1983.

Peter Eustace, 'Strategies for Product Success', *The Engineer*, 26 Jan. 1984.

Lawrence G. Franko, *The Threat of Japanese Multinationals*, John Wiley, Chichester, 1983.

Ronald Goodman and Richard S. Ruch, 'In the image of the CEO', *Public Relations Journal*, February 1981.

Christopher Lorenz, 'Many chief executives have surrendered control over innovation', *Financial Times*, 2 March 1984.

Alistair Mant, *The Leaders We Deserve*, Martin Robertson, Oxford, 1983.

P.R. Mills, Ed., *Managing for Profit*, McGraw-Hill, Maidenhead, 1982.

Thomas J. Peters and Robert H. Waterman Jr, *In Search of Excellence*, Harper & Row, New York, 1982.

Goronwy Rees, *St Michael: A history of Marks and Spencer*, Weidenfeld & Nicolson, London, 1969.

Andrew Robertson, 'Where Innovation Can Hurt', *Chief Executive*, March 1984.

Edgar H. Schein, 'The Role of the Founder in Creating Organizational Culture', *Organisational Dynamics*, Summer 1983.

Paul Sparrow, *An Analysis of British Work Values*, Work & Society, 1983.

Theodore D. Weinshall and Yael-Anna Raveh, *Managing Growing Organizations*, John Wiley, Chichester, 1983.

Daniel Yankelovich and John Immerwahr, *Putting the Work Ethic to Work*, The Public Agenda Foundation, New York, 1983.

Peter Young, *Power of Speech; a history of Standard Telephones & Cables*, George Allen & Unwin, London, 1983.

Abraham Zaleznik, 'Managers and leaders: are they different?', *Harvard Business Review*, May–June 1977.

Index

Index